Oliver St. John Gogarty (1878–1957) was
educated at Stonyhurst, Oxford and Trinity
College, Dublin. Gogarty was a fellow of the
Royal College of Surgeons of Ireland and, like
W. B. Yeats, became one of the first Senators of
the Irish Free State.

His books, available in Sphere, include *As I Was
Going Down Sackville Street*, a racy tale of
Dublin life in the 1920s, *Rolling Down the Lea*,
Tumbling in the Hay and *It Isn't This Time Of
Year At All!*

Also by Oliver St. John Gogarty in Sphere Books:

ROLLING DOWN THE LEA
TUMBLING IN THE HAY
IT ISN'T THIS TIME OF YEAR AT ALL!
AS I WAS GOING DOWN SACKVILLE STREET

Intimations

OLIVER ST. JOHN GOGARTY

WITHDRAWN

SPHERE BOOKS LIMITED
London and Sydney

First published in Great Britain by
Sphere Books Ltd 1985
30–32 Gray's Inn Road, London WC1X 8JL
Copyright © 1950 by Oliver St. John Gogarty

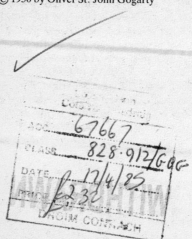
TRADE
MARK

Set in Times

Printed and bound in Great Britain by
Cox & Wyman Ltd, Reading

Acknowledgements

The publishers are indebted to *Town and Country* for permission to publish Doctors in Both Faculties, George Moore's Blackbird and George Moore's Ultimate Joke; to *Tomorrow* to publish The Wonder in the Word, Poets and Little Children, An Amazing Coincidence, The Life of Reilly and American Patrons and Irish Poets; to the *Atlantic Monthly* to publish The Enigma of Dean Swift. A Picture of Oscar Wilde was reprinted from the August 1945 *Esquire*, copyright 1945, Esquire, Inc. Green Thoughts, Let Us Now Praise Famous Men, The Most Magnificent of Snobs, Women with Charm, Can You Shoot in a Bow?, I Like to Remember, How the Poets Praised Women and Intimations were reprinted from *Vogue*, copyright the Condé Nast Publications, Inc.

Contents

DUBLINER
and OTHERS

Doctors In Both Faculties

James Joyce came loping across the path with a red oblong object under his arm. We met. I asked him what he was carrying. At once he assumed an air of almost ritualistic gravity, which was one of his ways of mocking outrageous fortune. With great seriousness we advanced toward the pawnshop. He passed a fine folio bound in red morocco over the counter. When the transaction was concluded, he turned with a sigh and said, 'That was Theophrastus von Hohenheim, called "Paracelsus"! He was doctor in both Faculties; and he never mentioned which was which.'

Doctor in both Faculties! How remote and cabalistic the title is! I recall it now because it is appropriate to so many medical men who owe their fame more to the Faculty of Letters than to the Faculty of Medicine; men who are so identified with literature that their connection with science will come to the reader as a mild surprise. Of such are Clemenceau, Chekhov, Swedenborg, Schnitzler, and the precocious genius, Otto Weininger – all within living memory. Of those of old there are many, but their relation to medicine is as obscure as was the science of their day. Two monks of the Middle Ages come to mind, Roger Bacon (1214–1294) and Rabelais (1490–1553). Both were 'doctors' and both are among the first-class intellects of all time. The first was the father of experimental science and a philosopher in the religious order of St Francis. The other, Dr François Rabelais, flounders in cap and bells with robust license through the Middle Ages, holding his dark lantern aloft and beaconing bravely onward toward the enlightened and untrammeled few whom he felt were sure to arise and assert the dignity and freedom of the human soul. The fools of his day regarded him as the fools of a later day regarded Shakespeare, as a 'smutster and punster' only. Rabelais made the world rock with laughter without knowing what it was laughing at – with laughter at humbug and at all the imbecilities of pomp, pretense, and false fame; laughter at himself caught in the human coil; laughter at 'what fools we mortals be'; laughter for

3

delight in very laughter, which itself is an assurance of a transcendental state from which something that is not mortal can regard mortality and, because of its own impassible nature, laugh.

It is hard to imagine the monk holding a general practice in his monastery. There is a legend of his practicing at Lyon. Yet he loved to air his knowledge of anatomy, such as it was in his time. Witness the description of the birth of Gargantua from his mother, Gargamelle:

'The cotyledons of her matrix were all loosened above, through which the child sprung up and leaped, and so entering into the vena cava did climb by the diaphragm even above her shoulders (where that vein divides itself into two), and, from thence taking his way towards the left side, issued forth at her left ear.'

In his discourse about borrowers he gives a long account of the functions of the heart and the physiology of the circulation; and he describes how carefully they sewed on the decapitated head of Epistemon so that he might give an account of his adventures in the underworld and allow the good doctor an opportunity for the greatest parody ever written at the expense of the great and powerful of this world.

The originality of the man! The devastating simplicity! The preposterous Odyssey to the Ringing Islands! Swift quarried from him. Balzac imitated his style. Whatever his claims to medicine may have been, Dr François Rabelais has cured the world from a mighty weight of melancholy. Cardinal du Belay was quite right in refusing to admit to his table anyone unacquainted with *the* book. Samuel Taylor Coleridge was the first in England to recognize the philosopher beneath the monstrosities and extravaganzas of Pantagruel. He was the first in England and the last.

Between these men of old time, when a bishop could confer a degree in medicine, and men of the times of Oliver Goldsmith and of Keats (who walked Guy's Hospital for twelve months) there must have been a great body of men who studied or practiced medicine and who wrote on other or allied themes. And so there was, but the writers do not rise readily to mind out of the Middle Ages because their writings were undistinguished or obscure – Lethean as their prescriptions were lethal – and were rapidly outmoded. It must be remembered that nothing changes sooner than medical practice and theories. At one period people are bled indiscriminately. At another (this time it is our turn) blood is being banked and transfused on a scale too nearly universal to be always justifiable.

Against this rule of thumb and the indiscriminate treatment of patients, one mighty figure rose at the beginning of the sixteenth century who, although he had not a medical degree, was a professor of Physic and Surgery at Basle. This was Philippus Aureolus Paracelsus, originally Theophrastus Bombastus von Hohenheim (1493–1541). He applied specific remedies in opium, sulphur, mercury, iron and arsenic to the treatment of disease. Medicine was dominated then by the writings Galen, Celsus, and Avicanna. If anyone's disease did not fit into one of these treatises, he was in a somewhat similar position to the present-day soldier who suffers from something which does not come under one of the categories in the army handbook. Paracelsus flew in the face of authority by denouncing the universal practice of blood-letting and purging. He treated a patient not as a 'case' but as an individual. He seems to have known that fifty per cent of all diseases are mental. Thus he became the first psychiatrist in Europe and a most successful doctor. After all, it is pleasanter to be treated as a human being rather than as a disease when you are ailing. Legend has it that the great humanist, Erasmus, was one of his patients. Paracelsus wrote *The Elixir of Life* and *The Philosopher's Stone* and he was Doctor in both Faculties.

It might be thought that we had emerged from the period of indefinite medical degrees and medieval occultism when we come to the time of Oliver Goldsmith, who is said by some to have had a degree in chemistry from Leiden, by others to have qualified as a doctor at Padua or Louvain. It is certain that he went to the University of Edinburgh. But his fame as a poet and playwright would have obscured a more certain record of his medical qualifications if such a record could be found. This 'very great man' (Dr Johnson), 'the most beloved of English writers' (Thackeray), the English Virgil, the sweet poet whom even the heroic couplet could not make dull, has buried his scalpel deep beneath his laurel bough. But medical degrees were not yet formal in Goldsmith's time. They were not very official even up to the time of Keats, who 'walked' a London hospital and was apprenticed to a surgeon until 1817. His connection with doctoring is remembered more by the infamous sneer of some arrogantly ignorant reviewer, a Scotsman, who advised him to 'stick to his gallipots' than by any reference to medicine the poet himself has made.

The 'faculty' which has beautified life and healed many from its cares is that which went to the writing of *Endymion*, *Hyperion*, and the great Odes.

Born while Keats was still alive, Oliver Wendell Holmes is so well known as a charming essayist that his connection with medicine is almost forgotten. Yet he was one of the foremost scientists of his day. His work on puerperal sepsis, repudiated as it was by contemporary authorities in England, happens to have been the correct interpretation of that disease. He arrived at his conclusions independently while Semmelweiss in Vienna was demonstrating the connection between infection and that of fever. He received his M. D. degree at Harvard in 1836 and he published his *Poems* the same year. Some men can blend medicines for the Muses. Oliver Wendell Holmes was the most successful of these. It may be asked why a man like Sir William Osler is not included in the same category as Dr Oliver Wendell Holmes. To include famous physicians who were also distinguished writers would open a lengthy list and require a paper all to itself, and it would depart from the subject of the present article, which deals only with those whose fame in the faculty of letters has left their competence, such as it was, in the other faculty, lost to light.

It is but to be expected that men who have become eminent through their medical training should possess a lucid, unequivocal, and precise style which would go a great part of the way towards genius did it not lack one thing, a thing so obvious that it is unnecessary to name it, a thing but for the lack of which every scientist and lawyer would be a literary genius instead of being, for the most part, cold as crystal or dry as a judge's joke.

These remarks do not, of course, apply to Sir William Osler whose many addresses and philosophical writings show not only imagination but a certain persuasiveness, as anyone who reads his *Aequanimitas* or his *Science and Immortality* will concede. The answer is that he achieved even greater distinction by his medical work in the Johns Hopkins University of Baltimore. On his record as a physician his fame depends. What an injustice would be done to his stature were this to be forgotten and his essays only to be remembered! To use a simile that may be somewhat disproportionate to the reverse of the case: it would be just as unfair to require that George

Bernard Shaw's reputation should rest only on the knowledge of medicine that his *Doctor's Dilemma* betrays. Osler was greater in the Faculty of Medicine than in the Faculty of Letters, just as he was greater as an American and a professor of Johns Hopkins than as a Canadian and a professor of McGill University. This, too, is true of his biographer, the eminent brain surgeon, Harvey Cushing, although his *Life of Sir William Osler* was awarded a Pulitzer Prize. And it applies with greater emphasis to Dr Crile, whose *Mechanistic View of War*, with its wonderful description of the utterly outworn and wounded soldiers during the retreat from Mons, sleeping a sleep so profound that they were cemented to the floor of a church by their own blood, would make the reputation of many a lesser writer.

Different, however, is the case of Alexis Carrel. He could tie a surgical knot in a matchbox with one hand, yet it was because of his *Man the Unknown* that he won popular fame, and not because of his unprecedented skill which brought him the Nobel Prize, or the fact that he rose up in his declining years and gave the benefit of his knowledge (and his life) to the children of France.

If Poetry be the crown of literature, then Robert Bridges, the late Poet Laureate of England, is the most eminent of the men who transcended medicine. For a time he worked as a country doctor in the vicinity of Oxford, where afterwards he lived in comfortable circumstances to a ripe old age. Never once, except for one, and that a very recondite, allusion, does he refer to his reason for abandoning medicine for the service of the Muses. He felt that he was a better poet than a doctor. He says as much in paying tribute to those physicists who devote their lives to research among the stubborn secrets of Nature:

> Thrice happy he, the rare
> Prometheus, who can play
> With hidden things, and lay
> New Realms of Nature bare.
> *That highest gift of all*
> Since crabbed Fate did flood
> My heart with sluggish blood,
> I look not mine to call.

He has in mind the line of Virgil, *Felix qui potuit rerum cognoscere causas*, and the one that follows it. He holds the opinion that theirs is a higher gift who can benefit mankind more directly and more generally by scientific discovery than by the inspiration of poetry. In fine, Dr Fleming, the man who worked with the 'hidden things,' the moulds and mycocytes, has, so far as mankind at large is concerned, a 'higher gift' than Shakespeare. Bridges thought that to lay Nature bare was better than to hold the mirror up to her.

In the little town of Hastings, where the battle of that name took place, a doctor trained in Edinburgh came to develop a country practice. For some time Dr Arthur Conan Doyle worked among the inhabitants of this Sussex town, where reigns a conservatism that goes back to the year 1066. Someone persuaded Conan Doyle to give up his efforts to become a popular doctor. Why not set up in London as an eye specialist? This he did with only slight success. For a little time he made a living by doing refraction work for his more eminent colleagues. It was obvious that he could not hope to succeed in London without the private means necessary to sustain a man until he can make a name for himself. His empty waiting-room gave him cause for reflection. He reflected. He still kept in mind one of his teachers in the Edinburgh Medical School, where he was a student – Dr Bell, Professor of Anatomy. Dr Bell had an extern clinic where he treated outpatients and taught his class. One day an upstanding man came to the clinic for treatment. He wore a cheap suit of clothes which was new and neat. He spoke in low tones, in a soft voice with respect for authority. This seemed all the more strange because he did not remove his hat in the presence of Dr Bell. He was suffering from elephantiasis in its preliminary stage. When he had gone, Dr Bell addressed his class:

'Gentlemen, the man we have just seen has been only recently discharged from the army. He kept his hat on because to him it is still part of the uniform he has very lately discarded. His clothes were new. His soft voice tells me that he belonged to a Highland regiment and that he has been stationed in the West Indies, for that is where he contracted his disease.'

All this turned out to be perfectly true. The impression it made on Conan Doyle was profound. From Dr Bell the inductive method of the greatest detective in fiction is derived. Dr Watson, his foil, may be considered to be Conan Doyle, laughing at himself. There is a lot of Irish blood in Conan Doyle.

8

The literary skill of this author is liable to be overlooked in the interest of the *Adventures*. But where can there be a better preparation for some dangerous and moving excursion than the midnight quiet of Baker Street when Dr Watson is making up his notes of the day's cases? The serenity of the atmosphere is suddenly dispelled by the ringing of the bell, a bell which has continued to ring in the pages of every detective story ever since *Beeton's Christmas Annual* gave Sherlock Holmes to the world. Thus Conan Doyle exchanged his opthalmoscope for the pocket lens of Sherlock Holmes.

English readers hardly can be expected to know how many prodigies of literary excellence forsook the practice of medicine in foreign countries. Only those of international reputation come to our ears. Outstanding among these is Anton Pavlovich Chekhov.

He began a medical practice, but tuberculosis put an end to a career which would necessarily engage him in hardships. He took to the less strenuous life of the playwright and the story teller. If there be any traces of the doctor of medicine in his writings, it is to be found in his attitude toward, rather than in any definite account of, the tragedy and pathos of human existence, the inevitable separateness and solitude of each human soul, the misunderstandings which arise in life.

He was born in 1860, two years before the great Austrian, Arthur Schnitzler, who outlived him by twenty-seven years, the author of *Anatol; None But the Brave; Fraulein Else*. Unlike the bulk of doctors distinguished in literature he employs his medical knowledge in delineation of character with a tendency to dwell on their pathological neuroses. This must appear to be a very inadequate estimate of a writer who held the attention of his country and of Europe for many years. It is almost inevitable that works read only in translation should by the loss of the rhythm, flavor, and associations of the original language somewhat diminish the stature of the writer. This applies more to Chekhov than to any other author, but it may to some extent be remedied by testifying to the greatness and humanity of the man which no translation can obscure.

Twelve years ago Dr Axel Munthe was being entertained in London because of the popularity his book *The Story of San Michele* achieved for him. It did this chiefly because the avowed intention of the author was to devote the proceeds to

9

a bird sanctuary on the Island of Capri. He was still being entertained in spite of the rumor that only the proceeds from the Swedish edition were set aside for the sanctuary. The British Lion is very often only a feted foreigner. Like George Bernard Shaw, who left Dublin to become an Irishman, Munthe went to London to become a lion.

As an example of creative literature the doctor's book may be discounted. It was more of the best selling than the best reading kind. Happily its success may have secured the author and the public from his medical practice.

Ireland, in addition to Dr Goldsmith, had two other illustrious medical authors; Bram Stoker, the author of *Dracula*, which is almost a word in the language, and, less well known now, Dr Charles Lever, the author of the very entertaining novels *Tom Burke of Ours* and *Harry Lorrequer*.

It is pleasant to think that the best writer of our time is an English doctor living in the United States. So famous has his writing made him that he is completely associated with literature and not at all with medicine, which he hardly, if ever, practiced. Somerset Maugham's works, with the possible exception of *Liza of Lambeth*, which may be autobiographical to the extent that it was derived from his medical experiences, are necessarily dramatizations of life. The superficial may not see below the surface and may retain the impression that Maugham is sophisticated and cynical. But no author can achieve greatness by superficiality or cynicism. Deep down for those who have the organ to perceive it, there is tenderness and an understanding of human nature which make Maugham the most significant writer of our day. Style has disappeared from contemporary writing. There is hardly a writer who can be recognized from his style. He is known only from his name on the publishers' blurb. This means that anyone can offer writing to the public with the lamentable corollary that the public can be molded to accept anything served up to them with the fanfare of advertisement.

For a realization of the breadth and erudition of Somerset Maugham, nothing can be more apt than a study of his *Introduction to English and American Authors*. In this anthology the clarity of his prose and the perception of his criticism are to be found; and with them a liberal education in contemporary literature.

Francis Brett Young is a meticulous exponent of prose. He

may be termed a stylist in that in his novels he adheres to the best traditions in the use of the English language. With him may be coupled the name of Hans Zinsser who wrote *Rats, Lice and History* in prose (appropriately) and *Spring, Summer, and Autumn* in verse, and best of all his own biography in *The Biography of R.S.*

William Carlos Williams has endeared himself to thousands by his poetry. And to those who go to the movies which, unhappily (or happily) make fame ephemeral, the name of A.J. Cronin is familiar through *The Citadel*.

If these are doctors who have achieved more eminence through their writing than their medicine, what of doctors – and these the more numerous – who have subordinated a learned and lucid command of the English language to the use of their profession? The foremost of these is assuredly that great alumnus of Dublin University, Dr Whitly Stokes, the foremost physician of the middle of the nineteenth century, a man of great probity, whose lofty and noble mind was unremittently devoted to the service of his fellow men. But a review of the literary accomplishments of men such as Stokes and Osler is a subject for an article the converse of this. Nevertheless, it is due to Hippocrates to correct a mistranslation of one of his great aphorisms. His Greek suffered through its Latin translation. 'Ars longa' is not what he said. It was for the poet Chaucer correctly to translate it:

'The life so short *the craft* so long to learn.'

Looking back through the history of medicine with regard to those who achieved fame in spite of it, the question arises, was it in spite of it? And an inquiry as to the causes that led men to forsake the most honorable of professions may be of some interest.

The first cause obviously is inclination, character. This in Darwin's case is history. Who, gazing at his bronze statue outside Shrewsbury – domed head, bearded face looking out from the days of unpressed trousers from under an inscription in Greek, 'I am, therefore I shall be' – would realize that in spite of his father's wishes he left the medical schools of Edinburgh to become a clergyman? Is there not some cryptic cynicism in 'I am, therefore I shall be?' If the words were intended by the sculptor to be put in the mouth of an ape and not a clergyman, there would be 'I am an ape, therefore I shall be – an ape.' 'Darwin's Theory,' as it is called, is doomed to perpetual misunderstanding. Dr Vincent Hurley declares that when he sees a crab driving a taxi down Park Avenue he will believe in evolution. That would convince even Dayton, Tennessee.

But to return to the reasons for relinquishing 'that highest gift of all.' In addition to disinclination there is the delay and difficulty of success. These beset, as has been shown, Conan Doyle. Then, not every man has the strength of character and the perseverance required for the seven years' servitude to study and to what amounts to the acquisition of a foreign language, in the preliminaries to a medical degree. Disinclination to bend the mind on inflexible facts; the recoil from a science which is consistent with many things but not with a 'fine frenzy,' particularly in an appendectomy or in the compounding of a prescription. Then there is 'the wrong of unsightly things,' the revolt against spending a life as it were in the green room and not in the front seats of the play. The recoil from ugliness. Probably these were the reasons why the poets Goldsmith and Bridges abandoned the directer service of mankind. Yet, after all, to the man who is whole there should not be anything inconsistent with a study which embraces all Nature and a life devoted to interpreting Nature in exaltation. Phoebus Apollo was God of Medicine, Music and Song. Nevertheless the fact emerges with the consistency of a rule that the more a man succeeded in the one faculty the less he mentioned the other.

George Moore's Blackbird

The scene for this story was set by George Moore himself, in his description of his garden in Ely Place. He lived in the fourth house of five in one of those delightful cul-de-sacs where peace reigns amid the subdued turmoil of an old residential town. The garden, entered by a little wicket at the far end of the cul-de-sac, had two walls. The one opposite the houses was covered by a spreading fig tree; the other was hidden by a wilderness of lilacs and ash trees. A third boundary was formed by the flank of my house, which looked out on the green expanse under George Moore's apple trees.

Perhaps once a week he could be seen strolling under the trees. He never appeared until about five in the evening, after his day's work of dictation, correction, reiteration, alteration, and exasperation. And you might be sure that he never appeared until, as he put it, 'the strain of composition' had left his face.

You could feel his presence, for it was out of keeping with an old-world garden. Looking like a boulevardier in his blue suit with its peg-top trousers, and his bowler hat, and always carrying a light Malacca cane, he would walk up and down inspecting the work of his gardener who mowed the lawn and attended to the reluctant flowers once a week. The denizens of the other four houses and I watched his perambulation. When he thought that he had been sufficiently observed, he would leave the garden for a stroll through the town.

So you see him walking on his lawn as if it were a rood or two snatched from the Champs Elysees, instead of a green oasis of the eighteenth century. His yellow mustache, and his pink and white porcelain face with the parrotlike, pale-blue eyes that could smile kindly only on a little child, appeared under apple blossoms which were not more pink and white than he. If you wish to hear him tell about his garden walks, here is what he says:

And wandering across my greensward, I came to my apple

tree now in bridal attire; not a petal fallen yet, but to-morrow or the day after the grass will be covered with them. . . . My garden is but a rood, and the only beauty it can boast of is its grass and its apple trees – one tree is as large as a house under whose boughs I might dine in the summer time. It is the biggest apple tree in all Ireland. A blackbird sings in it all the summer time.

That was written in the middle of the time of this story. How he came to meet the blackbird concerns us now.

One day he was startled by a cackling and flurry of wings among the lilacs. Carefully he parted the branches here and there with his cane. At last he spied, tail-tilting, ready to fly, the 'yellow tawny bill,' yellow as his own, and the pert eye of a blackbird that had flown over houses and walls to the garden. Evidently it was about to nest there. What a theme for an author – a blackbird in the heart of the city contrasted with the noise and insecurity without. And now he had frightened the bird away, perhaps forever.

For many days he forebore to walk in the garden, but he could be seen peering from his window for the blackbird.

One morning, early in the dawn or just before it, he heard the mellow notes. All his life he had been a poor sleeper; but now he could sleep well, for he had the long, sweet notes to waken him at dawn. It was his own bird – the bird that had come to seek the sanctuary of his garden. He would see that it was kept secure and unfrightened. The wicket gate was prompt-ly equipped with a chain and padlock, for small boys had been known to open the old lock with a knife about the time the apples ripened. As there was no other way in, the padlock would keep the gate secure.

He told his friends about his good fortune. Among his friends was Yeats the poet, a formal friend, but one whom Moore disliked. Moore disliked most of his friends, and they reciprocated, but Yeats he particularly disliked, for he felt Yeats would outlive him in fame.

Yeats prided himself in knowing more about wild things than Moore. Yeats announced that cats, not small boys, were the real enemy. Moore, who took 'no notice of what that fellow, Yeats, has to say,' nevertheless filled the pockets of his dressing gown – a red robe that cardinalized him in spite of himself – with stones to pelt at any cat that dared to trespass.

This was duly reported to Yeats, who was greatly amused. His comment, which he had related to Moore, was: 'Cats are nocturnal animals.' This was too much, and worst of all, it was indisputable. Even if Moore could dispense with the little sleep he snatched, what good would any missile be against cats in the dark? For days he meditated on Yeats and cats until they became indistinguishable in their hostility to both bird and Moore. He took counsel with his housekeeper, who suggested that he set a trap for the cat.

Meanwhile, just in case of an accident, I took care to let my cantankerous and unreasonable friend know that my house sheltered neither cat nor dog.

Some of the townsfolk used to wander into Ely Place on Sundays, look into the forgotten garden, and wander off. This became a menace to the bird in Moore's imagination, but as a landlord, he knew only too well that any attempts to curtail liberty in Ireland are followed by redoubled assertions of it. So he bore with the infrequent visitations, but counteracted them by making the presence of the blackbird a great secret. By this means he thought to prevent the story from spreading.

Of course it spread. The unpoetic inhabitants of Ely Place took it for granted that the bird came from the adjoining Green; but the spent poets and disgruntled authors said that Moore had imported it from Moore Hall, and that it was about all that the Land Commission had left any landowner in the country.

Another precaution against stray cats took the shape of a wire fence, which was added to the walls and railing of the garden. The cost of this crept into Moore's face and style: he looked peevish, and his brother, the Colonel, came in for more abuse in the third volume of a trilogy he was working on than in the first two. As for me, I noticed it in another way. Through no fault of mine except in forgetting that 'eternal vigilance is the price of freedom,' I ran into him one afternoon. He passed me with a nod then, turning suddenly, hailed me and said solemnly, 'If you would refrain from sunning yourself in the windows overlooking my garden, you would greatly oblige me.'

'What's the idea?'

'I have asked you to oblige me, that's all.'

I resented this request to keep away from my windows when Moore was most of the time at his. After dinner that night Yeats came to see me. We talked and smoked for a while.

15

Yeats seemed somewhat preoccupied, but there was no use in questioning so intelligent a man – in his own good time he would come around to whatever was on his mind. After a long interval, he asked nonchalantly, apropos of nothing, 'Have you a cat in this house?'

'I don't think so,' I said.

Yeats seemed disappointed. I should have left it at that, but I had to tell him all about Moore's blackbird, even though I knew he was keeping himself thoroughly informed. Then I added, 'Moore asked me today to keep from the best side of my house.'

'For what reason?'

'He's afraid that I will frighten the blackbird, and that he will fly away.'

Yeats pondered. 'Moore should have known that the bird must have made a survey of the locality before deciding to nest in it. He must have seen your windows long ago.'

He fell silent. The only way of interesting Yeats in anything was to connect it with the ancient sagas of the land. Presently I said. 'One would think from all the fuss he is making that Moore is the only one in Ireland who has ever listened to a blackbird singing. You remember the quotation from the early Gaelic, "The music Finn loved was the song of the blackbird of Letterlee?"'

Yeats brightened at once. 'Yes, and you remember the hermit who wrote a marginal note on some manuscript, telling what delight the blackbird's song was to him?'

'But why is Moore doing this to me?'

'Moore wants to identify himself with the blackbird, so that he may be associated with sweet song.'

'A quite unsuitable association for Moore, because the blackbird was called the Bird of Valor by the ancient Irish, who used them to fight instead of gamecocks. Moore is not remarkable for valor.'

Yeats was amused. I then told him of the elaborate precautions Moore had taken to preserve the life of the bird, not omitting to mention the trap for cats.

'A cat?' Yeats became meditative. Then he changed the subject so abruptly that I knew he was impressed.

Evidently Moore's efforts to preserve his songster were effective, for the bird sang in the garden until almost the end of summer. One day sometime before his song should have ended for the year, I missed the sound of him in the garden. Day followed day, and yet no note. There was no sign of Moore either. Ely Place seemed deserted until Yeats came around again. He was bursting with information.

'Do you know what happened to Moore's blackbird?' he asked.

'No,' I said.

'He caught it in his own trap!'

In this manifold life of ours I have found that there are times when no comment at all is wiser than the most edifying discourse. In silence I moved the ash tray nearer to my beaming friend.

George Moore's Ultimate Joke

Most funerals are boring and uneventful – at least in this world. The mind refuses to cherish them and dismisses them as gloomy and unproductive memories. Some funerals can be tragic when they touch our affections. On the other hand there are desirable funerals such as those I would willingly stand one or two people I have met through no fault of my own, though the cortege were expensive and the catafalque beyond my means. But I am glad to say that those whom I wish to see lying in state are gradually becoming fewer and fewer as time wears on and I grow as sweet and mellow as an old maple tree. I am content to leave them alive and give them scope to 'do their best,' which is about the nastiest predicament in which a worthless fellow may find himself.

Taking them all in all, there are few funerals to which we can look back with a smile, yet there is one which I will always remember with pleasure, not because I was not sorry for its subject, but because of the diversion it provided and because I had a shrewd idea that the principal intended it, as he had intended so many actions of his life, to be an embarrassing jest. This was the funeral of George Moore, which, on the whole, I enjoyed more than any other funeral I ever attended.

It may be said to have started in my Dublin house in Ely Place, so I will begin the tale from there.

Colonel Maurice Moore had come to announce his brother's death and to invite me to the obsequies. This was quite a compliment, for it included me in the very small group outside members of the family who were asked to attend. The Colonel, with his high, narrow, aristocratic forehead, looked exactly like the description given of him by his brother George: 'Maurice entered the room looking like a Spanish grandee.' He motioned me to a seat and sat down himself. Deliberately he searched for his pince-nez, then desisted, and said with solemn severity, 'I have something to say to you.'

This made me extremely uneasy. I began to feel guilty in an obscure way, doubtless from my long association with George, who was always at loggerheads with his brother. I felt as a soldier must feel when he is waiting for the verdict of a court-martial. The house seemed not to belong to me. I found the cause of this at last; the Colonel was sitting crosswise in front of the fireplace. He looked me full in the face: 'You know George is dead?'

Gravely I bowed my head.

'But there is something else which I must tell you. Until you hear it, do not say whether or not you will go to the funeral.'

Some awful skeleton in the family, I thought, but immediately I wondered how there could be one left which George had not gleefully exploited. For example, that insistence of his, which made the Colonel so indignant, that their father had committed suicide. That was one. There were others. And here, apparently, was some post-mortem scandal that George had bequeathed to his family. As I was steeling myself to hear the worst, the door opened and Mrs Kilkelly, the Colonel's aged sister, was announced. She had the Moore eye, as gray and as opaque as a parrot's, and skin the color of old lace which does not reflect the light. She had just arrived in the city, and had tracked the Colonel to my house.

The Colonel rose and greeted her shortly. They had been closely in touch by telegram since George's death. He waited until we were both attentive, then continued, 'As I was saying, George is dead.'

'We know that,' said his sister curtly.

The Colonel turned his head and regarded her in silence. 'But there is something worse,' he said.

'Worse?' she exclaimed. 'But what can be worse than death?' What indeed? I thought, and racked my brains to answer the question. There was, of course, dishonor; too long foreknow-ledge, as with a cancer; outliving all you love; misassociation; being beholden to someone you despise. Oh, there are many things worse than death, but we had yet to know which one the Colonel had in mind. At last he found his gold pince-nez. He tugged at his pocket and produced a paper.

Again his sister asked, 'What can be worse?'

'Cremation for a Catholic,' the Colonel answered gravely, and turned his head admonishingly toward his sister. 'Let me read you this.' His hand shook, not from agitation but from paralysis agitans.

'I am reading from his will. "My body to be cremated and my

ashes spread over Hampstead Heath where the donkeys graze.'"

There was silence for a moment.

'Maurice, we can't have this,' his sister asserted.

'I am afraid, dear, that it is too late. George has already had himself cremated.'

'But the ashes?'

'I have taken steps to stop that nonsense. I am crossing to London to-night. I shall return with the remains, the ashes. And he shall be interred at Moore Hall.'

As a rule, I am full of tact. I tried a little of it.

'There cannot be any hurry, now that the worst is over. Those undertakers are most obliging. They will do as they are told.' And my mind ran on suave Farrell, the Dublin undertaker, or mortician, as he would style himself now, who, in the days of the four-in-hand hearses, comforted a widow with, 'Quite a nice day for a funeral, Madame. Just enough wind gently to stir the plumes.'

I was brought back from Farrell and his plumed horses by the Colonel's looking steadily at me over his spectacles.

'The worst is not over by any means. For one thing, the Church will not countenance a pagan funeral, and, for another, the country people may attack the party and break the urn or whatever it is. That is why I hesitated before asking you to join our little group. As relatives, we may be more or less exempt from molestation, but . . . Anyway, I hold you under no obligation, although you were a friend of his.'

'But I shall be delighted,' I blurted out. 'Delighted' was not quite the word I wanted to use, not exactly *le mot juste*. 'By all means, I will go,' I said. 'We were next-door neighbors for years.'

'They cannot prevent a man from being buried on his own property,' Mrs Kilkelly said, forgetting that Moore Hall had been burned down during the Civil War, cremated like its owner, and that all the country people wanted was some excuse such as a show of religious indignation to cover their misdeeds.

'I am sure that is very loyal of you,' the Colonel said. 'I will let you know in due course when we are to meet at Moore Hall. We must be getting along now.'

He looked at his sister and together they left the room.

So George has done it again, I said to myself. 'Even in our ashes . . .' He knew quite well that his family would never permit his ashes to be scattered among the donkeys. The newspapers would be full of the scandal. No. Ashes to asses would never do.

It was some time before the word went around that George Moore's ashes were in Dublin. I was not concerned with the rumor, for I knew that the Colonel would keep his word and that I would be informed at the proper time. There was, as I had said, no hurry. Now that he had become 'a handful of gray ashes,' George had achieved a kind of immortality; he could undergo no further change. However hot the weather, he would keep.

It was Saturday when the telephone message came. The Colonel said, 'You see, as Moore Hall has been burned down, my sister and I intend to stay tonight at Balla. It is the nearest place with a hotel to Moore Hall. It is on the Westport Road. The only other Dublin man who is coming is Best. AE cannot attend.'

'Why?' I asked, astonished.

'For reasons of his own.'

'Very well, Colonel, I will be with you tonight at Balla.'

'Thank you,' said the Colonel formally.

Well, well, I said, when the Colonel had gone off the line. AE is not coming for reasons of his own. For all his moral courage, AE has never given his sails to the tempest. He refused to join the Senate. Now he jibs at George Moore's funeral. And they were such long friends. Maybe AE has not forgotten George's remarks about his lady secretary, which AE made him withdraw under pain of a lawsuit. Anyway, he has reasons of his own. So had Plato. 'Plato was sick' when they were waking Socrates, who had become unpopular with the Church, such as it was, in Athens in the days of old. The same thing over again. Oh, these philosophers! They spend their time with reasons of their own.

There are more roads in Ireland than in England, strange as it may seem. Eighteen thousand miles and more, well macadamized, that will take speed, and innumerable side roads that admit of many short cuts. I was in a hurry, but, like my friend, Dr Tyrrell, 'had no time for short cuts.'

After some hours, I reached the long street of the usual Irish village, with more houses on one side than the other, and I knew that I was in 'the wide plain of Mayo,' mother of great pugilists and policemen. On the left, near the end, was a large stone house, the only hotel in Balla. It was an old house, but, like all Irish hotels, was spotlessly clean within. The plain dinner was excellent but by no means as festive as a pagan funeral feast should be. There was no sign of Best. That surprised me. The tall, blond, unaging Best, whom Moore had described with affection – almost: where was he?

Best was one of those quiet, inoffensive, scholarly men who, for all their quiet, have plenty of guts. The chance of an attack on the hotel, or an attempt to break the urn could not have a deterrent effect on Best; nor could even the aftermath of a religious imbroglio. I looked at the empty place. The Colonel caught my eye: 'Best will be late. I will send a car to meet the train at Westport. If he is not on it, he will probably drive through the night. He will be here before morning, in plenty of time.' Thus spoke the Colonel, relying on Best.

There was a nervous feeling, not without stimulation, of tension in the air. I began to wish that I had not brought my car. It was rather conspicuous; and if there were any rioting, the zealots would take it out on inanimate objects as well as on us. At the moment it was safely locked up in the garage of the local magnate, who was also proprietor of the hotel. I went to take a look at it before going to bed.

On the way up through the long corridor to my room, I could see in front of the end window, outlined against the summer night, George Moore's sister sitting grimly upright with a rounded object held in her lap. She was taking no chances. She would entrust to no one her brother's urn. She determined to keep watch over it all through the night. I hoped that she would be safe in her territory, where the Moores had held sway for generations, where the first president of an Irish Republic went forth to meet the French landing at Kilalla in 1798. Besides, no Irishman raises his hand against a woman unless sanctioned by Holy Matrimony.

I must have either a good conscience or a bad memory, for I like to be alone with my own thoughts. I lay awake thinking of George's many affectations, his aestheticism with regard to art: how not very far away – in Westport, to be exact – while staying at the house of his land agent, one Ruttledge, he called out loudly for a bath towel. When informed that there was one in his room, he said that he knew that, but that he wanted another for he was using the first to hide an awful portrait of a woman, which, as one might guess, was the portrait of his host's wife. I thought of the way he used to 'lend' me his garden which was opposite his house and flanked mine. I was to pay the gardener as well as the rent. As a parting shot he made the proviso that I was to give no garden parties in it during his absence for he 'could not bear to think of housemaids crossing his lawn with pots of tea.' Then his choosing Avignon for a love affair, the home of the Popes. He died ripe; he was over eighty. And he never made a woman unhappy. Eighty years: ten such lives as his would bring us back to an Ireland before the Norman invasion, which happened about 1172. Twenty Moores, and we would be back in Ireland before the coming of St Patrick. How near history seems to us when we measure it in life-lengths of old men. And thinking of Moores backwards, I fell asleep.

It is amazing how a good verse can rouse me more than wine. I woke repeating lines of James Stephens' magnificent reincarnation of blind Raftery's 'County of Mayo,' with its wonderful rendering of the internal assonances:

I say and swear my heart leaps
    up like the rising of the tide,
Rising like the rising wind till fog
    and mist must go,
When I remember Carra and Gallen
    close beside;
And the gap of the Two Bushes
    and the wide plain of Mayo.

Framed between the Two Bushes! And it was on Castle Island in Lough Carra that we were going to bury George.

At breakfast silence seemed to have fallen upon the hotel. There was no one about to whom orders could be given. The servants probably were all at Mass. Yet that could not altogether account for the desertion of the place, for there had been an early Mass which the Colonel attended, and even the last Mass must be over by now.

As the Colonel, who was in charge, did not show any surprise at the servants' defection, it was no business of mine to comment.

He rose, and with his napkin in his hand like a lowered flag, he addressed me: 'You will take my sister to the lake. She will show you the way.'

By the time I had the car round, Mrs Kilkelly was waiting. She was draped and clothed in black. I knew by the bulge

23

behind her long veil that it was the Urn she held. She looked about as happy as Electra full of good intentions towards her brother. I helped her into the car.

It would have been more dignified if we had had someone to drive us; but there was not a soul in sight. Yes; if we had Farrell's four-in-hand, how majestically they would have swept through the gates of Moore Hall and up the pleached drive that was all but overgrown. Yet, perhaps, it would look somewhat ostentatious to have four horses drawing a little pot.

There was not a soul in sight as we drove along. Surely, I thought, they are waiting in ambush for us heroically behind a hedge or a high wall, ready to lie to the last man, if surprised by the police. So I feared; and the fear, if it did nothing else, served to depress me into the right mood for a funeral, a mood you are apt to get into especially when you think that the funeral may be your own.

'George is to be buried on Castle Island,' my passenger announced. The sealed orders were being revealed!

'The Castle Island he mentioned in *The Lake*?' I inquired eagerly, charmed by the poetry of the thought of burying him on an island in the Lake he loved. After all, in spite of his soldiering, the Colonel is a bit of poet. There is poetry in all the old Irish families – poetry and romance.

'I am unaware of any other island in Lough Carra,' she said.

'*The Lake* is not one of his best books,' I remarked, after a pause, to let her see that I missed her snub. I thought that I would get a bit of my own back, so to speak. *The Lake*, save for its description of Lough Carra, might have been written by a mischievous and petulant child. George, without asking my permission, had made use of my name for his hero, and the hero (a priest of course, to annoy the Colonel) makes an ass of himself with some schoolteacher, housemaid, or lady's maid. I cannot be sure. I never read my friends' books. Anyway, George showed his dearth of power to draw characters. The letters the priest writes to his paramour and the letters she writes back are by the same hand and might just as well have been written by a professional letter writer.

'It should never have been written,' I heard her say grimly.

'Will I drive down over the lawn?' I asked, now that the full expanse of the lake opened through the trees on her left.

24

'There is no other path.'

'I was thinking of the jolting,' I said, but my solicitude was more for the urn than the choephore.

By the gravelly margin of lovely Lough Carra two boats were drawn up. The nearer was a small boat that could easily be managed with two oars. Eighty yards off there was a larger boat that looked to be waterlogged from where we stood. It would require two men to row it. I turned to the boat near by. It lay with its prow in the water and its stern on the gravel.

'Is there no one to row us over to the Island?'

'I understand that you are quite able to row.'

There was nothing for it. I cast a glance at the island shimmering on the lambent water. I could see the gray keep rising above the trees. 'Be gallant and do your best,' I admonished myself, though it was – what? – thirty or thirty-five years since I had rowed a boat.

Launching presented a problem. I had to get the urn-bearer in and yet have the boat near enough to the water to launch it. I pushed it three-quarters into the lake leaving the stern with its seat within reach of the lady. I helped her in as best I could seeing that it was risky to take her by the arm.

'I am sorry,' I said, 'but I will have to leap in beside you for a moment before I go forward and trust to my weight to get her off.'

At last we were afloat and my task all but accomplished.

'One would have thought that the Colonel would have got one of the old hands from Moore Hall to row us over,' I ventured.

'They were forbidden to.'

'Forbidden? By whom?' I asked puzzled.

'By the parish priest.'

I saw it all in a flash. The Colonel's diplomacy and the parish priest's tact. The Colonel must have explained his predicament; and the priest, who knew how devout he was, obligingly denounced the funeral and ordered it to be boycotted. That explained at once why we were neglected and yet unmolested.

So far so good. We were halfway over. I looked around. The Castle and its island had disappeared. My bewilderment did not escape my passenger.

'It is over there,' and she inclined her head in a direction over my right shoulder. I must have been steering for the gap of the Two Bushes – anywhere but Castle Island. Encouraged by being given a bearing, I took off my silk hat and laid it under the seat where it would be unlikely to fill with water if I caught a crab. The heat was stifling. I felt as if I were developing a goiter. Forgetting my passenger, I took off my frock coat. I pulled in silence in my shirt-sleeves. My hands were peeling. Foolishly I dipped them in the water to cool them. It made them worse. I blamed the heat for most of my troubles and I removed my waistcoat. I recalled Frank Sugg, the cricket coach at school, who used to advise us, 'Open your shoulders.' Evidently my shoulders were open now and the bulging of the muscles or the fat or whatever it was tightened my braces to an uncomfortable degree.

'I trust you will not think it necessary to divest yourself of any more apparel.'

I had forgotten the old lady in my agony. She stared at me as cheerless as an empty grate.

'Oh, I'm exremely sorry. I know it's an odd way to go to a funeral.'

'Very!' was all she said.

I could see the urn clearly now, for the sun shone through her veil. It was made of dark red clay with a raised ornament in the form of a festoon that encircled it under the neck. A reproduction from our Late Bronze Age. If the Colonel had had it made in Dublin, it would account for the delay in these obsequies. But it may have been an original from a cromlech somewhere in County Mayo or in Moore Hall.

I was rowing evenly now. By grasping the oars tightly I numbed the pain in my hands. I saw the urn glow at me again, and I suddenly thought how the owner of the ashes must be laughing at me, a victim of his ultimate joke. Charon, by gad! I said. He has turned me into a Charon to row his shade across this Lethean Lake. How he must laugh at me now. Perspiring and in pain, without even an obol to pay for the ferrying. Little did I think of what I was letting myself in for when I volunteered to row across Lough Carra the ashes of our George. Charon! Well, I'll be . . . All right, my old Carrain guest, if I may call you so, I'll land you soon now. I looked over my shoulder for the fiftieth time. I could make out the window slits of the square keep of the Castle deep in foliage, and two men like workmen standing on the shore beside a little wall. But the Colonel and Best where nowhere to be seen.

'Where is the Colonel?' I asked.

For answer I heard a noise like a machine gun. The gray face looked towards Moore Hall; there was a group of about eight people in the larger boat rapidly approaching propelled by an outboard motor, which, as I learned later, was the property of the local doctor. Another boat was in tow. Even at the distance I could make out the Colonel and Best with the light on his golden hair. The Colonel had conducted the campaign fault-lessly up to this. The doctor, probably on account of his association with death, was exempted from the ban against the funeral of George Moore. But why was not I included in the boat with the motor? I forebore to ask. I worked it out like this: in most funerals it is the custom that the corpse goes first and no one must precede the hearse, no more than a rider should over-run the hounds in a fox hunt. So I, the chief surviving friend, with the chief mourner, who had got all the obols under her brother's will (as it later transpired), were told off by the Colonel to lead the sad procession.

'The boat is drifting.'

'Only for a moment, I am putting on my clothes.'

I gave the little craft a final thrust that would have shot her half ashore, and probably spilt Mrs Kilkelly, had not ready hands been there to take the prow.

There was much whispering and closing of the ranks. At last we were all arranged about a little square of stone masonry two feet high which walled in a square opening as deep again as the wall was high. Into this cyst the urn was carefully laid by the Colonel.

That was not the end. It was the beginning of the 'service.' I, who had never attended a Bronze Age funeral, was somewhat at a loss as to procedure. But the Colonel knew it all. Best was motioned forward, and he took his place beside the little tomb. He had a paper with an oration by AE from which he read. I wondered how AE would work his perverse friend into the number of the nation's heroes. Hush! Best is reading:

'It would be unseemly that the ashes of George Moore should be interred here and the ritual of any orthodoxy spoken over him; but I think he who exercised so fantastic an imagina-tion in his life would have been pleased at the fantasy which led his family and his friends to give him an urn burial in this lake island which was familiar to him from childhood. Whatever be the fate of his spirit, it cannot be the fate of the Laodicean, he who was always hot or cold. There could be no fitting burial for

27

one who always acted from his own will and his own center in cemeteries where the faithful to convention lie side by side.

'However he warred with the ideals of his nation, he knew it was his Irish ancestry gave him the faculties which made him one of the most talented and unfilial of Ireland's children. His ironic spirit would have been pleased at this urn burial in this lonely lake island, so that he might be to Ireland in death what he had been in life, remote and defiant of its faiths and movements. He loved the land even if he did not love the nation. Yet his enmities even made his nation to be as admired and loved as the praise of patriots. He had the speech of the artist which men remember while they forget the indiscriminating voices which had nothing but love.

'If his ashes have any sentience, they will feel at home here, for the colors of Carra lake remained in his memory when many of his other affections had passed. It is possible that the artist's love of earth, rock, water, and sky is an act of worship. It is possible that faithfulness to art is an acceptable service. That worship, that service were his.

'If any would condemn him for creed of theirs he assailed, let them be certain first that they labored for their ideals as faithfully as he had for his. He left his family and his country for his art and because of his art his family have brought his ashes back.'

As the devoted sentences rose into the air it seemed as if AE were offering a sacrifice to the shade of his departed friend.

The words ceased to ascend. The Colonel came forward to address those 'who had come the long distance from Dublin or London to honor by their presence the last remains of George Moore, buried, as is right, in his ancestral demesne within sight of the house in which he was born, and the tombs of his ancestors . . . For the method of his funeral I will only say that it goes back to the early years of Ireland's civilization, to the Bronze Age, a thousand years or more before the Christian era, when Ireland was the richest and most cultured country in Western Europe and traded even as far as Palentine before the time of Solomon.'

In the bright sun with bared heads we listened to the Colonel. He read from a paper which shook, but the shaking gave emphasis to his words. The paper rose and fell and flashed till it looked like the sword of some Homeric hero defending the body of his fallen comrade. But in the course of his oration the panegyric veered to praise of the urn – 'From our best ceramic period, when ours was an expanding civilization and Irish art and Irish arms were recognized over the known world.' His enthusiasm for the urn was making him forget the contents! 'One has but to look at this urn with its severe simplicity, barely relieved by the ornament that encircles it, to realize the artistic height to which our country had risen long before the Christian era, long before the contaminating influences of Britain reached our shores.'

You do not applaud a funeral oration but, at the conclusion, I was so filled with admiration for ancient Ireland that I looked around for an Englishman to fight. There were two strangers, but they had cameras and were probably members of the ubiquitous press. As there were no dissenters, the funeral threatened to end peacefully.

The men were filling the cavity that held the urn with cement. Fussily the Colonel turned from side to side. His light-colored eyes glared at me, but the sun was in them and they passed me by.

'Is there no Christian symbol to be found at all?' he demanded. His sister remained unmoved. Suddenly a black board appeared, about a yard square. On it was a white cross made by the meeting of the tips of four isosceles triangles with the bases out – the cross the St John's ambulance people use. The Colonel directed it so that it should be seen. It was held in position; and I heard the cameras click.

The funeral party faded away. I had already taken up a good position in the motor boat. I spent the time of the return journey gazing in rapture at the waters of the lake. Liquid gold, liquid ecstasy! I have seen the Blue Grotto under the Island of Capri where the waters look as if the moon were dissolved in azure; but the waters of Lough Carra were more wonderful because I little expected a miracle, a miracle of beauty at a pagan funeral. Moore Hall took the sun now and again over the mile of wine-light water. Its cremated walls rose dark against the darker circle of its woods.

The funeral had been a great success. Nobody had dropped dead to cast a gloom on the proceedings. It had touched the two pinnacles of life, beauty and excitement. I returned to the city 'smiling that things had gone so well.'

A Picture of Oscar Wilde

Fifty years after the downfall of Oscar Wilde, the screen production of two of his stories (*The Canterville Ghost* and *The Picture of Dorian Gray*) and the fact that nearly all his writings are still in print, seem to give a clear indication of the abiding quality of his genius.

'If such characters really exist in Dublin,' said Bernard Shaw on reading a book by James Joyce, 'there should be a Commission to inquire: Why?'

Not only do such 'characters' exist in Dublin, but they have been there for two hundred years, from Dean Swift to Bernard Shaw, who is one of them himself. Another of them was Sir William Wilde, father of the subject of this article.

Dublin is a city out of the Eighteenth Century, adorned by beautiful and spacious squares bordered with lilac, hawthorn and laburnum behind their iron railings. On each side stand stately houses of rose-red brick in front of which, in the days of Wilde's childhood, rows of cabs awaited a call or carriages moved up and down. These were the houses of the 'nobility and gentry.'

Number One Merrion Square, one of the largest of the squares, was the residence of Sir William Wilde, a man of immense energy and appetites, the famous aurist, oculist and archeologist. When a modern surgeon is operating for mastoid disease, the first incision he makes is 'Wilde's incision.' As an eye doctor Sir William is not so fixed in history; but there is a story which is told of him today, that when a rich patient expostulated at Sir William's charges for removing his eye, Sir William said, 'My good man, it took me a hatful of eyes before I could do what I have done for you.' Which goes to show that one has to pay for experience.

His were the pioneering studies in the heroic sagas of Ireland which led to the Gaelic revival. From these sagas came the names with which he named his famous son: Oscar Fingal O'Flahertie Wills Wilde; Oscar was the Irish Hector, the son of the Irish poet-warrior Ossian, who was the son of Fingal or Finn.

His admiration for the O'Flahertie, one of the princes of Connemara (a lovely mountainous district by the Western ocean), led Sir William to call his son after him as well as after the heroes of thousands of years ago; and also to buy a beautiful lodge or 'camp' on an isle in Lough Fee in the heart of Connemara. It is known as Lady Wilde's Island. But to return to Dublin, where Wilde got his wit.

Eighty years ago there was a caste system in Dublin as defined as that in Montreal or Quebec. The educated and the wealthy formed a coterie which included nobility, gentry and the professional classes of medicine and the law. Medicine and law never flourished more successfully than in Oscar Wilde's Dublin. The great doctors entertained each other and dined out almost every night with judges, lawyers or eminent government officials. Wit and anecdote circulated with the port. The reception rooms of the lofty houses were almost as fine as those in the Provost's House. Lady Wilde, with earrings to her shoulders, held her salons and wrote patriotic poems for *The Nation*. Those poems were not altogether approved by the aristocratic and therefore conservative elements of the city, but then allowances must be made, for Lady Wilde, who called herself Speranza, was undoubtedly 'a little queer.'

The sallies to which young Oscar listened were such as these: Sir William Harcourt was blackballed by one of the exclusive Dublin clubs. His remark on hearing the result: 'It's quite a nice club – only for the members,' went the rounds and can be traced in the wit of Oscar, which often depends, like that of Shaw, on inversion. Another citizen, well known for his wit and shrew of a wife, lay dying and answered with a smile when a friend asked him how he was: 'Hovering between *wife* and death.'

One of the doctors, who was a great trencherman and host, was afflicted by a superabundance of flesh seen only once in a century. He must have weighed close on six hundred pounds. He drove about in a 'fly' or hansom cab imported from London. The street arabs could not resist: 'Dr Meldon, lend us your belly for the next picnic!' And the wits propounded the quiz: 'What is more wonderful than Jonah in the whale's belly? Dr Meldon in a fly!'

In one of the houses almost directly opposite to that of Sir William, another famous surgeon and resident of 'the Shadow of the Valley of Death,' as Merrion Square was called, got himself involved in divorce proceedings with the wife of a dentist. It was bad enough to bring notoriety of this unsavory kind on oneself, but with the wife of a dentist! That was a breach of the caste system, reprehensible and unedifying. The dentist charged that the surgeon took his wife in a cab for a drive one night through the leafy lanes of Dublin's suburbs. There was much wrangling in court as to whether misconduct was possible in a cab. The Dublin cabbies rose in importance. They felt proud of being a part of such notoriety. A year later, when the surgeon was leaving church with a young bride on his arm, about to go on his honeymoon, a cabbie approached and, saluting with a whip adorned with a knot of white satin, offered his services: 'Cab, sir?'

Dublin blazed with another scandal. This time the principal was Sir William Wilde himself. Rumor had it that one of his lady patients accused him of misconduct. It was never cleared up. The public, full of faith in human frailty, believed the worst.

Trinity College, with its park, groves, gardens and athletic grounds, occupies the center of the city. Its gates almost touch the gardens of Merrion Square. The Fellows of Trinity had an immense influence in forming the opinions of aristocratic society. Trinity had educated most of the men who ruled the country at the time and it held itself superior to Oxford and Cambridge.

Upon two 'dons,' or Fellows, the fame of the College depended in young Wilde's day. One was the Rev. John Pentland Mahaffy. The other, Dr Robert Yelverton Tyrrell, professor of Greek. Naturally the men were rivals.

Mahaffy had an enormous influence on the growing Wilde, more than has ever been suspected by his biographers or pornographers. He was a magnificent figure of a man, physically and mentally. One of the greatest scholars of his century, he stood well over six feet. With a broad forehead, auburn hair that turned into two close ear-whiskers, wide generous lips and shrewd eyes, he looked like the personification of all the dons who ever walked a college cloister. He had that rare thing, a perfect musical ear. He was a good judge of claret and cigars. He enjoyed the acquaintance of many kings and talked to them as an equal. In fact his rival, Dr Tyrrell, was well aware of this foible and used to quote:

'The King of Assyria was drinking himself drunk in his tent

with the four and twenty kings who were with him and who were helping him.' Then he would add innocently, 'I think that our friend Mahaffy would not have refused a little light refreshment in that society.'

Dr Tyrrell anticipated criticism by making no pretences to abstinence. 'Is it true, as the Archbishop says, that you got drunk at his dinner table?' 'Oh, no, I took the obvious precaution of coming drunk.'

Mahaffy practiced what the Greeks call *eutrapelia*, that is, the justifiable arrogance of the well-bred. The effect of this on the susceptible Wilde may be imagined. It made him arrogant without justification.

In 1877 they both went on a visit to Greece. The trip through Greece and the meeting with the King did little good for any humility a youth should have. Oscar heard his Master correct the King:

'I am afraid Your Majesty is laboring under a misapprehension. These tunnels are not catacombs. The Greeks were never so barbarous. They are entrances to silver mines. Plato, for all we know, may have been a profiteer.'

On their return to Dublin they were fined for outstaying the leave of absence. And Mahaffy was forbidden to preach in the college chapel because of a sermon, or rather a lecture, he delivered to the students on his *Rambles and Studies in Greece*. 'I never could quite forgive St Paul. There was an excellent university at Antioch. He never once availed himself of it. Never!'

When Dr Tyrrell heard that Mahaffy was forbidden to deliver any more sermons he complained to his friends: 'Since Mahaffy has been silenced, I am suffering from insomnia in church.'

What biographer has realized the influence of such an atmosphere on the development of Oscar Wilde?

As Mahaffy says: 'The inevitable never happens in Ireland, the unexpected always.' And what could be more unexpected than that one morning Mahaffy should say to his disciple: 'You are not quite good enough for us here, Oscar. Better go to Oxford.'

What lay behind that we shall never know. Mahaffy was a shrewd judge of men.

At this time Oxford was about the worst place for a neo-pagan and poseur. It provided a stage and what Oscar wanted –

33

limelight. A stage whereupon to practice his interpretation of Mahaffy's disdain. But he could not quite 'get away with it,' though he went very far, for he had neither the authority, the wisdom nor the grandeur of his precepter.

But he brought to Oxford a whole battery of Dublin's quips and quirks. When asked why, with his seemingly powerful physique, he did not take up rowing and join one of the College eights that were practicing and training on the Thames, he replied: 'I don't see the use of going down backwards to Iffley every evening.'

Among the mistakes he made, a fundamental one, was to think that anyone can transport the wit of Dublin to an English city. Ireland abounds in wit which is explosive and cruel. England has humor which bespeaks the toleration of a people who believe that they are above vicissitude. When vicissitude does come it brings out their humor, which is more or less unconscious, for it consists of a revelation of an attitude toward life. It is somewhat of an anachronism to jump forward to the present time in order to give an illustration of English humor at its best, but maybe it is justifiable.

An old housewife in London was carrying home some things for Christmas during the blackout. Suddenly the alert sounded and she dropped her parcels in the dark. After some time, when the all-clear came on, she groped for them and gathered them up with the remark: 'I wish this 'ere 'Itler would marry and settle down.'

How radically different this is from the amusement that comes from the perversion of some well-known saw, such as 'He who hesitates is lost,' which Wilde turned, Dublin-fashion, into 'She who hesitates is won.'

Or 'Thick as thieves in Vallambrosa.'

Well, he walked amongst the sophisticated. Walter Pater was trying to 'burn with a hard gem-like flame' not very far down 'The High' from Oscar's college, Magdalen. And there were very many of the aesthetic set ready to sit at Pater's feet. But he 'dwelt apart.'

Wilde worked hard at Oxford despite the temptations to mingle with the lordlings. Some he knew would avoid him, for their sole interest was in horses. Knowing this he gave utterance to his well-known description of an English fox hunt: 'The pursuit of the uneatable by the unspeakable.'

With one lordling he formed a fatal friendship. Yes; he

worked hard. He won the Newdigate, the prize the University gives annually for English poetry; and he composed most of the poems that were later published when he went to live in London. But the outstanding example of his genius was the idea, conceived in Oxford, of his novel *The Picture of Dorian Gray*, which is to my mind the greatest symbolic story ever told.

He graduated at Oxford, taking a first in 'Greats,' which is not only a fine intellectual achievement, but an Open Sesame to society, as well as an assurance of high-grade employment.

Well had Mahaffy said with his supercilious and somewhat cynical humor: 'If you want to get on in London society, go to Greece and come back and tell them about it.' Oscar had been to Greece. His scholarly attainments at Oxford were further evidence that he knew Greek; and he who knows Greek is a gentleman. Every drawing room that was becoming something like a salon in Victoria's days of official dullness welcomed the young Alcibiades. His newly published poems ran into several editions, and that is pretty good for poetry, even in England where they make it, or made it once upon a time when that time included giants such as Tennyson, Swinburne, Browning, George Meredith, Rosetti and William Morris. Oscar, though overshadowed by the gravity of Browning, was well able to turn the charging bull inside with a banderilla: 'Meredith is a prose Browning. So is Browning.' Pages of criticism in a phrase.

He was an undergraduate all his life. He never grew up. His poetry never got beyond a college 'quad' or a drawing room, or the verse that Blackwell of Oxford publishes at the expense of budding bards. And yet his lines to *Theocritus* and his ode to *The New Helen* are among the finest of their kind in the English language.

The Picture of Dorian Gray! It came like a comet and was the talk of the town. Its provocative preface set forth his attitude towards life, which was that of a patrician to the decadence of ancient Rome. He wore a fringe like that of the Emperor Nero; and indeed his wit and terseness in packing reams of criticism in a few words likened him to Nero's arbiter of the elegances, Petronius. Just as did Caesar Borgia, Wilde modeled himself on the greatest and most blasé decadent the world has known. But his ideas of the elegances were extravagant. In a land of understatement he was an exaggeration.

He dressed like a continental tenor or a successful dealer in antiques who has been exalted to the peerage. He was in a sense a dealer in antiques, for he sold a store of the ancient classics to an astonished public. In the age of Nero he would have been entirely probable; but in Victorian London he was an anachronism. He invented yellow shoes; and we are wearing them. He decried long trousers, which were designed to cover the swollen ankles of one of the Georgian kings, the Fourth probably; and he uncovered his own long, fleshy and unathletic calves by going back to knee breeches.

But it needs money, even if only cab fare, to bask in the drawing rooms of London. And Oscar's money, the little his father had to leave after a life of entertainment in Dublin, was running out. He decided to go to the United States on a lecture tour. When asked at the customs if he had anything to declare, he answered, 'Only my genius.' He stayed an unusually long time in America and, unlike Dickens, he did not turn sour or ungrateful to a country that had enriched him, even though his lectures were somewhat premature.

Back in London he settled down and produced play after successful play. He lived luxuriously and entertained as his father entertained in his native city. Never were plays such as Wilde's seen on the London stage. Wilde did not confine himself to the stage but made a stage out of London, with himself as the only hero. He departed far from the Greek maxim: *Nothing too much*. 'Nothing succeeds like excess.' The light on the surface hid and still hides the greatness of the man. It concealed from the critics the fact that a new departure had been made in drama. Here was a man from Dublin more brilliant than his forerunner, Richard Brinsley Sheridan. Swift, Burke, Goldsmith, Sheridan and Wilde! What a nurse of genius, Dublin!

William Butler Yeats (another Dublin man), himself a great conversationalist, said that Wilde was the greatest talker he ever met. He could disarm and charm even when surrounded by envious enemies who would invoke the massed might of all the righteous dullards to destroy him. He had outraged all London. His brilliance was bad form and his inversions of accepted opinions were insufferable! 'An honest God's the noblest work of man.' Was he to be permitted to undermine the morals of a country whose morality depends on hiding, if not suppressing, immorality? He was publicly flaunting vice in their faces. The sky fell.

The sordid details and indefensible acts of the trial are better left to the pornographers who dwell on this side only of Oscar Wilde. Some held that he was badly advised by legal counsel, others that he was handicapped by the fact that he did not know how much the prosecuting attorney, Carson, an old Trinity College man, knew of his career in Dublin. This recalls Mahaffy's 'You are not good enough for us here.'

Ill-advised or not, quips and smart answers will not defend a culprit from the deadly ritual of the law. And even had Wilde been exculpated, there was within him an heredity that would have arraigned him again. He out-scandalized his father's scandal. His friends deserted him, all but a few, and Robert Ross. A yacht was waiting for him if he decided to fly. Yeats, who always gave a man the benefit of romance, saw in this stand of Wilde, and in his refusal to run, the spirit of the duelist, the man of honor.

However it be, even the years in Reading Gaol could not make him sincere, for he returned when he was released to his minion in Italy. Poverty-stricken and sick from meningitis caused by a mastoid condition which even 'Wilde's incision' could not adequately relieve, he passed away in an obscure lodging in Paris with the old light smile on his lips that could never be extinguished.

'I am afraid that I am dying as I have lived, beyond my means,' he said when the landlord's bill was presented.

Flippant, superficial, facetious, a spoilt schoolboy? Very well; but what other attributes are there for the Spirit of Wit, this Puck? Would you have him Victorian? Wilde could not have been as successful had he been graver or more sincere. England, that insists on her poets having a bad conscience, or on preaching, cannot make a laureate out of a lyricist: Francois Villon would have never left Reading Gaol.

It is to the subconscious nature one must go if there is to be an assessment of the greatness of Wilde. His superficiality was his way of expressing his art. He was, not without a deep significance, attracted to Nero, who died proclaiming himself an artifex, a playboy. His was an Ariel-like attitude to life. But his prophetic soul was capable of assessing himself and leaving on record his own testimony in his *The Picture of Dorian Gray*. He knew what was happening to him. He could not lift a hand to prevent it without slaying himself. Just as Shelley was able to prophesy his own stormy death in the end of *Adonais*, so Wilde wrote early in life an account of what his end would be. Only natures of supreme genius have this prophetic power. Those with an eye to see can read it all in his esoteric testament and apologia, *The Picture of Dorian Gray*.

Some years ago there was talk in Dublin (when isn't there?) about bringing his bones back to his native city. What good his bones would do a town that needs another wit like his is not apparent. Maybe, if we judge by the appearance and dress of some of the officials, the place has become a mortician's parlor. In Dublin, with its censorship on books, Wilde would be dead beyond redemption. He is buried more appropriately in Père Lachaise.

James Joyce As A Tenor

Shelbourne Road is about two miles from the center of Dublin. It runs from Ballsbridge, past the Veterinary College and the wall of Beggars' Bush Barracks, and ends at the busy intersection of the road to Irishtown. At the Ballsbridge end there is a laundry abutting on the River Dodder; at the other end, a pleasant public house. There are houses, all two stories, but on one side only. The other side is blanked by the barracks wall built of the black-gray Dublin limestone that seems always to be crumbling. It is a quiet road. The only traffic consists of the usual milk cart with its 'gradual' horse, a laundry 'float' or two and, now and then, the Sanitary Corporation's scavenging cart full of liquid mud.

The long day is silent in Shelbourne Road; the quiet is suitable to a poet or a musician.

In Number 60, the only house in the road with a trellised porch, James Joyce hired a room in 1903, the large room on the first floor. It had two windows looking out on the wall of the barracks and was as broad as the width of the house. He also hired a grand piano from Piggott's, the musical depot in Grafton Street. Very likely his uncle, who worked as a clerk in an attorney's office and knew the ropes, had told him that he might count on six or seven weeks before the piano could be seized by Piggott and Sons for his failure to pay installments. And six weeks would give him time to practice for the National Song Festival, the Feis.

Meanwhile, the piano had to be installed. As tips were a consideration, it was decided that Joyce would be out at the time of the delivery. I, who was useful on such occasions, was told to watch from a vantage point and to report when all was clear. We were to meet at the end of the road.

All went well. The piano, legless in transition, was carried sideways through the door. After a considerable interval the men emerged and, gazing about for a while, lit their pipes and then reluctantly drove away empty handed. Joyce had won the first round. Six weeks later he won third place at the singing competition. He might have won first place in his class, but apparently sight reading embarrassed him even as a youth, though he never complained about his eyes to me. I never saw him wearing spectacles. However, he seldom took me into his confidence. He did inform me that he had thrown his prize-winning medal, a bronze one, into the River Liffey. It was useless for barter.

I heard him sing one morning when I called at Shelbourne Road. His voice was clarion clear and though high pitched was not at all strident. His build may have been too slight for a successful tenor. I remember John McCormack, whose career began with a victory at the Feis, telling me that he could not reduce below 224 pounds without a change in the quality of his voice.

Joyce was full of original ideas. He planned to have Dolmetch make him a lute. Then he planned to visit the coast towns of England during the summer holidays and there sing sea shanties and the old ballads of England. There is a letter written to me in 1904 which may be seen in the New York Public Library in which he mentions this idea. It anticipated by forty years the balladists of the present day. One of his songs was:

Farewell and Adieu to you,
    Spanish Ladies.
Farewell and Adieu to you,
    ladies of Spain,
For we've received orders to sail
    for Old England;
But we hope that we one day
    may meet you again.

He sang another about the Green Cuffs, a fifteenth-century regiment of militia:

The Green Cuffs are comin' in, Dollie, Dollie.
That will make the lassies sing, Dollie, ah!
Dollie dey dil and do. Dollie, Dollie,
Dollie dey dil and do. Dollie ah!

I think the song actually ran, 'The Green Cuffs *is* comin' in.' Joyce was very particular about the text. It ended by a mention of a girl who must have been the first *vivandière* in history:

40

Dollie Coxon's pawned her shirt
To ride upon the baggage cart.

The newspapers gave Joyce good reviews of his singing at the Feis. He kept the clippings in his pocket until they were reduced to powder. He must have wanted them for advertisments of some sort to help his projected tour because he wrote to the poet, Seumas O'Sullivan, to send him some typewritten copies. He took care to parody O'Sullivan's recently published poem, *Praise*. Joyce evidently was too proud to ask without the parody, which enabled him to feel more like a patron than a suppliant. *Praise* goes like this:

Dear, they are praising your beauty,
    The grass and the sky:
The sky in a silence of wonder
    The grass in a sigh.

I too would sing for your praising,
    Dearest, had I
Speech as the whispering grass
    Or the silent sky.

Joyce's request in the form of a parody went:

Dear, I am asking a favor
    Little enough;
That thou wouldst entype me
    This powdery puff.

I had not heart for your troubling,
    Dearest, did I
Duly possess a type-writer
    Or money to buy.

His ear for rhythm was infallible. This is a very different thing from an ear for music. According to the French poet, Josè Maria de Herèdia, '*La musique des poètes n'a aucun rapport avec la musique des musiciens.*' Joyce was one of the comparatively few poets who were musical in the musician's sense. Yeats was tone deaf; so by deduction was Byron; so was Burns; but Joyce was gifted with a double ear, exquisite in both faculties. His first volume of poetry, *Chamber Music*, is one proof. The other is his success as a singer.

* * *

Strange, almost incredible as it may seem now to his admirers, Joyce was more intent on becoming a singer than a writer. Although he competed at the Feis long before he conceived *Ulysses*, he was devoted all his life to music. This is borne out by the the story of Joyce's projection of himself into the person of Denis Sullivan, a prominent Irish-American tenor of the beginning of the Century.

At the age of eight Sullivan left County Cork with his parents and emigrated to the United States. Later he toured Europe as a tenor and in due course his tour brought him to Dublin, where he sang in that empty booth which was called the Royal University. It was only a building where students from all parts of the country came for examinations in the subjects for which the Royal University held a charter. Joyce and I were both members of the Univeristy, although it had no dormitories and was unused most of the year. During the empty periods it was often rented out as an opera house. To this building in Earlsfort Terrace Denis Sullivan came. He sang in *William Tell* and attracted considerable notice even in Dublin by his achievement in taking a very high head note in that opera. He was a man of magnificent physique; but like many good singers, he was a bad actor.

While he was performing in Dublin I lost track of Joyce. I never connected Sullivan's presence with Joyce's absence. Little did I know that Joyce had found a hero who was not himself – at least, not directly; but as it transpired later, it was in the character of Denis Sullivan that Stephen Hero came into his own and dominated the scene. While Sullivan was being praised, Joyce was vicariously happy. When Sullivan's star declined, Joyce raged, for he saw in the decline of his idol nothing less than a universal conspiracy of envy and ignorance, not unlike the conspiracy that he imagined was directed against himself. This persecution obsession is curious and should not be lost sight of in any psychological study of Joyce. He thought that Sullivan's lack of success was an index of the blindness, or rather the deafness of the general public. Joyce attributed Sullivan's failure to make the Scala in Milan to the apathy of Margaret Burke Sheridan, the most famous cantatrice of her time, who was the Scala's principal artiste. When we discussed this matter she said to me, 'Sullivan was not a man that one could do things for. He expected the Scala people to come to him.' She spoke almost apologetically, as if to justify her conduct against Joyce's charges. Her need for justification I took to be evidence of Joyce's persistence in what amounted to an *idée fixe*, one of his most prominent characteristics. Witness the unremitting labor he put into the writing of *Ulysses* when there was no hope of the manuscript ever seeing its way into print. He persisted in championing Denis Sullivan although the tenor had already found his level of success. Sullivan acquired a considerable income in the provinces, even if he did not appear in the greatest theater of all.

Margaret Sheridan is a very generous soul. It was undoubtedly because of her influence that Sullivan was engaged for twelve operas in Covent Garden, London. But as Margaret Sheridan says, 'You cannot build an opera on one head note.' Nevertheless, Sullivan was well advertised and the great day of his first appearance in Covent Garden drew near. As luck would have it, or perhaps because of the resources of the management, Their Majesties intimated that they would be graciously pleased to attend. Thus the first night of the opera became a 'command performance,' and the theatre was duly packed by the loyal subjects of the King and Queen.

It is very difficult for Americans to realize the importance and significance of a 'command performance' in London. Any actor who is held worthy to appear or to be 'commanded' to appear before the King and Queen is 'made.' The management must have been in a dither and their sense of judgement upset for Sullivan's performance. They chose *Gli Ugonotti* rather than *William Tell*. Perhaps Joyce was right for once, and there may have been a conspiracy against the American to prevent him from stealing the show with his high note in *William Tell*. It may be that they calculated that any note penetrating the royal heads would cause too favorable an impression and – with due reverence be it spoken – an undiscriminating or an insufficiently discriminating opinion in favor of an American, and an Irish-American to boot.

I like to think that anyone who appears on the stage before Their Majesties is 'made,' for there is a remnant of the magical in this notion. The conductor of the orchestra or the director of the ballet would be persons better qualified to judge the merits of a performer rather than the King or Queen, who conceivably might be asleep; nevertheless, asleep or awake, the King is infallible in music or ballet. To him is attributed the 'lucky eyeball' of an ancient Irish king in one of Yeats' unpublished poems. Denis Sullivan had reached the summit of his success in Europe when he was 'commanded' to appear. He would be beheld by the thousands, looking upon the same actor as Their Majesties. And appear he did. There was six feet two of him in that magnificent figure of a man. No matter how many Guards regiments Her Majesty had reviewed, here was the equal of any man in them. He broke into song. Before half the first act was over, Their Majesties graciously rose and left the royal box and Covent Garden. What an outrage and insult both to Ireland and America! Let no one deceive himself with the surmise that Their Majesties were not fully aware of the significance of their action. Wars have been caused by lesser insults. It is the business of Their Majesties to be aware of the importance of their simplest public actions. They are the English nation personified. They walked out on Ireland, America, and James Joyce. Joyce consequently came rushing from Paris. He entered Covent Garden Theatre in the middle of a performance and asked to see the manager. He was abusive and loudmouthed. Margaret Sheridan was told to calm him; but he would listen to no entreaties. 'You call this an opera? It is a WC (water closet),' he shouted. I am indebted to Miss Sheridan for this account. If I had been at the meeting, Joyce, I have no doubt, would have employed his favorite oath: 'God eternally blast and damn!'

After the disastrous performance, Sullivan received the customary registered letter cancelling the contract for the eleven operas he was to sing and his salary. Margaret Sheridan's representations influenced the management to give Sullivan his contract fees, but they did not permit him to appear again. Considered from this point in time, it does look as if Joyce was partly right and that there was, at least in this instance, a conspiracy against Sullivan who was more or less Miss Sheridan's nominee.

In Paris Joyce provided two rows of seats, paying for them out of his own pocket, for those who wished to bear him out and hear for themselves what a great singer the Fates were conspiring against. Joyce saw in Sullivan the victim of a fateful conspiracy. The truth was that Joyce himself was the Fates' victim. He was treated badly by a Dublin publisher; 'suppressor' would be perhaps a more appropriate name for 'Maunsell's manager.' But then Joyce was always treated badly by life, which threatened him with failing sight and darkness prema-

44

turely, turned him into a lonely antagonist and alienated from humanity the gigantic powers that he possessed. He got a bad deal from his father; and so it was all the more necessary that he compensate for the defections of his parent. To use the language of the psychiatrist, Joyce saw in Denis Sullivan a 'father image,' and he saw himself as the Crowned One (Stephanos), the Hero he would be. He therefore installed Denis Sullivan in his restricted House of Fame along with Dante, St Thomas Aquinas, St Augustine, Ibsen, and himself visualized as Sullivan-Joyce.

Joyce was an unlovable and lonely man, but he willed his life. He was an artist deliberately and naturally, and for this he sacrificed everything, even his humanity. But he made a grave mistake in his conception of an *artist*. He imagined, filled as he was with ingrown French ideas, that an artist was someone detached from humanity – an observer, and an inhuman one at that. This dehumanization plus a lack of decent reticence (a trait of Dublin as well as of mental homes) and a persecution complex roused in him an indignation which enabled him to scrawl – as it were, on the dead walls of the city – the most indecent graffito of decadence ever written: his *Ulysses*. With it he smeared with farce the grandest story ever written in verse.

He had the wrong idea of an artist when he dressed himself as Arthur Rimbaud and sent postcards with his portrait from Paris to his friends – or rather to his acquaintances, for he would not acknowledge that anyone could be his friend.

He was the self-styled *artist*. In the great periods of production of imaginative forms there was no such thing as that. Phidias never knew he was an 'artist'; neither did Praxiteles. While Leonardo da Vinci thought of himself as a military engineer.

Joyce was an ascetic. This statement may be as hard to accept as the statement that Joyce thought more of himself as a singer than as a writer; nevertheless, it is true. His rare bouts were part of his defiance and his rebellion against life. He never escaped from the prison built about him in Ireland, the mediaeval Church. It had made him an ascetic. I always felt that he was out of place when he dealt with love. There was something affected, tolerant and artificial about the few love songs that he sang. He must have been influenced in favor of music by seeing it, as he did during his school years, as a part of the religious ritual which influenced him profoundly. There are tones and semi-tones and rhythms all through the prose of *Ulysses* that are echoes of church music, plain song and chant. These may be discounted. It is more the *musique des poètes* carried into writing, rather than the music of musicians, that concerns me.

Did he join in the chapel of his school? This is for those interested in his life to discover. Some day I expect to see a commentary of Joyce containing a list of all the mentions of music, song or dance. In his words the dance will come into the commentary because the compiler will have ascertained that Joyce practiced ballet dancing in Paris. I was glad to hear that Joyce did so; it is proof that he had snatched some hours of happiness from a life that treated him none too well, in spite of his fame. 'To be happy is the chiefest prize,' the greatest lyric poet of all sang. And I like to think of Joyce when I knew him as a carefree student who had written *Chamber Music* before his nineteenth year and recited his poems to me in a garden near Glasnevin, or hired a grand piano to practice for the Feis. I think that he derived more happiness from his voice than from his writing.

Like Huysmans, Joyce might have been affected by the tenebrous terror of Church music, had there not been the earlier conditioning. He heard singing in his nursery and nature had endowed him with a musical ear. Thus the very susceptible stage of adolescence was not really a period of gloom for him. But instead of a musician he became a rebel, the first literary anarchist in Europe, and blasted and damned eternally all conventions. Anterior to all the stages of his life which brought him fame, however, was the period when he was Joyce the singer of carols, old ballads and sea shanties. All he wanted was a lute made by Dolmetch and the proper English audiences.

The Most Magnificent of Snobs

The word 'snob' is said to come from "s. nob." a contraction of the Latin words, *sine nobilitate*, which was the term used in the exclusive, lordly schools of England to describe a student who was not the son of a nobleman. It is easy to imagine how the untitled scholars, in trying to ape their more privileged school mates, assumed the airs and affectations which we associate with a snob.

There have been three or four outstanding examples of the snob in the last two centuries. Beau Brummel was the greatest snob of his time. You may remember how one day the Beau when cut dead by George IV, that corpulent king, asked the monarch's companion, 'Who is your fat friend?' He outsoared all snobs by that remark and he deserved to be identified with that which he affected to be, a gentleman, a paragon of fashion and a wit. What tailor's son could pretend to be unacquainted with his king?

Oscar Wilde was another kind of snob. He assumed an attitude of well-bred arrogance without the breeding that could carry it off. No one would call Wilde a gentleman. Matthew Arnold was a snob whom everyone could. By becoming an Inspector of Schools and having to be an example to so many school boys, he ultimately became identified with his pose. In fact he became such an exemplary gentleman that he felt constrained to jilt, having kissed her, a governess because 'she was not quite a lady.' It would seem that school masters *ipso facto* must be snobs.

A snob is a society poseur who affects a status to which his birth or his worth have not entitled him.

Now let us examine the medium which is most favorable to snobs. It must be a civilization in which nice class distinctions exist – nobility, titled persons, landed gentry, the Church, the Judiciary, the professions – upper, middle and lower classes and tradesmen. Below these the abyss.

Such conditions can exist only where there is a Court, for there only (if we except the Republic of Liberia where there is a Duc du Marmalade) are titles and honors derived from the Crown. The court of K. K. Emperor Franz Joseph in Vienna was rife with snobs. There nearly everyone had a title, even down to the girl in the newspaper kiosk. In England you will find people so desirous of titles that, if they cannot acquire them, they will stick two surnames together with an hyphen, for example the Storr-Smiths; the Bruce-Bruces; the Porter-Yapps; the Brook-Acres and so on. The professional classes have so hyphenated themselves that a special order of knighthood was instituted to preserve Christian names.

If you find snobbery like this in the shadow of a genuine Court, what must it be where the Court is an imitation one? That you would say would be the place to find the most marvellous snobs. Of course it would be. It was. I have lived half my life in it. In Dublin we had only a representative of the King, a Vice-Regent and a second-hand Court. The Vice-Regent was called the Lord Lieutenant. He lived in the Vice-Regal Lodge and held his court in Dublin Castle. If Hell is paved with good intentions, Dublin was paved with great affectations. I knew nearly all of them. Show me your company! I hear you exclaim. You are right. I was one; but the pose wore thin and went off when the tinsel court disappeared.

But what scenes when the Dublin 'season' began! The town filled up with carriages revealing girls dressed like brides. These were the debutantes of the country about to be 'presented' at court. What attitudinizing weeks before the 'season' opened! Class distinctions were drawn tighter. The doctor's wife became somewhat nonchalant in her recognition of the wife of the dentist. The dentist's wife hardly recognized the wife of the attorney. She in her turn grew less affable with the grocer, especially if there were other customers about. 'Have them delivered!' No one would put a cabbage in her bag. The wife of the judge had to fall back on her lorgnettes to perceive any citizens at all, which action was declared by the wife of Jack Lalor, the barber, to be sheer snobbery.

But it was great fun. If Lord Wimbourne was Lord Lieutenant, there was sure to be good polo in Phoenix Park between the officers of the various cavalry regiments (fresh ponies for every chukker). Lord Dudley, who in his day was just as open-handed, attracted all the 'nobility and fashion' to the half-dozen race tracks which ring the city; or presided over what was reputed to be the biggest horse-show in the world from the Royal Enclosure on the Grand Stand. When the Scotsman, Lord Aberdeen, was appointed, there was a 'heavy change,' not in coin, but in liberality. He and his wife economized in every way. It was the custom of the Lord Lieutenant to kiss each debutante as she was presented, a survival of the *Droit du Seigneur*; but even this went in Aberdeen's day; not from halitosis but from the intervention of his wife.

When at last they left for Canada, they took nearly everything out of the country with them except its tuberculosis.

But where in all this medley of display and pretence is the most magnificent snob you ever met? I am coming to him now. I had to show his environment to do justice to the man for truly he rose superior to it all.

While not Scots' parsimony (for there are very generous Scotsmen) but the parsimony of the Aberdeens was degrading the idea of monarchy in Dublin, there reigned, aloof from all the tawdry entourage, in the beautiful Georgian Provost's House of Trinity College, its Provost, the Reverend Sir John Pentland Mahaffy. He did not attend Dublin Castle. He held a court of his own which dominated intellectual Dublin. He set the fashion in opinion and diffused a desire for distinction in manners and good taste. The circle was small; but in it was all that was graceful and intelligent in the town. He was great in stature as well as in mind. He had that thing, rare in a generation, a perfect musical ear. From the Silent Sister, which is the name by which Trinity College is known among the other universities, he taught Cambridge and Oxford Greek. His works on the manners and customs of Greece and its lyric and dramatic poets are textbooks on the banks of the Isis and the Cam. As a scholar he was of international repute before the German 'specialist' drove the urbane scholars out of the schools.

Beyond the walls of the University amongst the majority of the townsfolk he appeared to be supercilious and affected. To his intimates he was a mentor, a friend, a philosopher and an *Arbiter Elegantiae*. His humor was sly, gently cynical and benignly sarcastic. It is told that once when travelling by train and sitting alone in one of those corridorless apartments, a dry-eyed, sepulchral fellow entered at the last moment as the train was moving out. Cornering the Provost, the man asked, 'Are you saved?' With his quizzical smile Mahaffy answered, 'To tell you the truth, my good fellow, I am. But it was by such a narrow squeak that it won't bear discussing.'

There are those who hate what they cannot assess. And Dublin was unable to estimate his greatness because it was apparent only to that selecter set that formed around him. To the citizens he appeared superior and supercilious as indeed he was; but they saw him thus because 'they had not worked under a master.' This was an expression he actually used when returning to me what I thought was an excellent essay, 'Pencraft,' by the late Sir William Watson:

> My dear friend,
> The whole thing is perfectly true. But I am afraid that the fellow has never worked under a master.

Truth, untutored, was at a discount.

The Dubliners could not understand him so they expressed their resentment against the superiority that they could sense by the only word in their somewhat limited vocabulary which they thought suitable. What else could he have been to those who were impressed by the tinsel court but a snob? Besides, these courtiers were sore because by the time the Aberdeens had made monarchy ridiculous, they were left without a platform from which to look down on their fellow citizens. So the snobs called him a snob.

Nothing makes people more malevolent than intimations of greatness which they can neither apprehend nor encompass. Any sign of superiority appears to such people as snobbishness. Only in this way does the Provost become the most magnificent snob I ever knew.

It is true that he was the friend and the guest of kings. Apart from the romance of it, it widens one's experience to visit a court; and Mahaffy wished to ascertain for himself those things that concern a crown. He could teach kings in his turn as Sir John Cheke 'Taught Cambridge and King Edward Greek.'

As might be expected from a courtier and a lover of great houses, the Provost was a Conservative. I remember after lunch in the beautiful gardens of Sir Horace Plunkett's house near Dublin, Mahaffy was walking towards a sheltered rosary to smoke a cigar for although 'Nobody but a boor smokes out of doors,' the windless bower excused him. He was overtaken by that impassioned philanthropist and hater of injustice, George Russell, better known as AE, who was working with Plunkett at the time and had met Mahaffy at lunch. The conversation turned on the repressive measures that were being employed by the Tsar. In accordance with his *Some Principles of the Art of Conversation* he could not encourage anyone to monopolize table talk. So Russell overtook him in the grounds: 'Sir John, Sir John, the Tsar is knouting them and sending them to Siberia. You should write to the Times and use your influence about it.'

'Now let us get this right, my good fellow. The Tsar is knouting whom?' Taken aback, Russell recovered and gasped,

'He is knouting the Russians of course.'

'Quite so. And if he doesn't knout them, they'll knout themselves.'

He certainly was a Conservative. If it has not appeared so far, it could be deduced from his objection to the policy of a member of Parliament, Swift McNeill, who was proud of his lineage:

'Let me see. Let me see. Swift McNeill?'

'Oh, Sir, you must know him. He is descended from Dean Swift.'

'By whom? Stella or Vanessa?'

And then the quizzical smile.

The Principles of the Art of Conversation may well become an historical document when the manners and customs of the commencement of our century come to be studied together with the culture with which they disappeared. It is written with headings and sub headings and all the arrangement and accuracy of a philosophical work which indeed it is. I went to the 42nd Street Library the other day to consult it only to find that though listed, it was missing. I have to rely on my memory for some of its doctrines. One was that each guest should contribute to the flow of soul. To another I have already referred: Under no circumstances should anyone try to monopolize conversation which should 'be kept in the middle.' How wise was that admonition. I have learned many times when some bore held up the table only to tell some stock story that might be anybody's property.

It is many years ago since I first saw the Provost. He was crossing a quadrangle between two gardens in the college front square. The awe of him kept me at a respectful distance. Some college youth or 'man' was angrily abusing another who was off stage. The Provost came upon him unawares and stood beside him smiling. The wild words ceased instantly. Later, I heard that the Provost mildly rebuked the youth.

51

'My dear fellow, you should not swear. By so doing you may lose your immortal soul, or, what is worse, be fined two and six pence.'

There was an English lady visitor in his house who hearing him give examples of that truly unique, compact and comminuted form of speech, the Irish bull (she was too dense to get it), asked rather contemptuously:

'Now what exactly *is* an Irish bull?'

'A male animal that is always pregnant, Madam.'

And his eyes smiled as they were wont to do when ignorance was discomfited.

The war of 1914 came on and his friend the Kaiser was an anathema. Some who did not like Mahaffy tried to embarrass him as he was speaking at a public function. 'What about Kaiser Bill?' they shouted. Mahaffy paused, turned and said blandly,

'Now that you mention it, I am afraid that my friend Kaiser William is making rather an ass of himself; but he is still quite the nicest emperor I know.'

Deliberately contemptuous, how could he but invite the only term of opprobrium they knew?

We were travelling to go fishing in the West of Ireland while the railway accommodation was curtailed and crowded. Some jockeys got into the first class compartment. They were complaining that they were out of work on account of the war. He sympathized with them and put them at their ease which was upset by the sight of his clerical collar. Soon they lost constraint and told him all their troubles. He amazed them by the knowledge of horses he displayed. He knew the pedigree of every race winner. They left regarding him with astonishment and admiration.

'What an absurdity,' he said to me. 'Why, the Greeks never put a ban on the free passage of jugglers and actors between their camps when at war. Why should these poor fellows be deprived of their livelihood?'

Subsequently, when fishing on a mountain lake he became expansive. He was tying a fly to a cast while I was making suggestions. 'Let us do nothing foolish.' That appeared to be his maxim. To the gilly who spoke Irish though his children did not he said, 'If they insist on teaching your children Irish, make them teach them the older language that existed before Gaelic of which only three or four words remain, the names of the two

52

rivers, Boyne and Shannon, and the name of the autumnal solstice. Anyone with a little application can learn them in a week.'

Claret was his drink and the drink of the generation that preceded him. One day at lunch he praised the claret and asked me where I had obtained it. I confessed that I had bought it at an auction. 'I never heard of such a thing. Laying down a cellar by hap-hazard. My friend, you are not worthy of your wine. I will send my man in to remove it.' And he did.

He was an authority on all that appertained to the palate. He thought that every substantial man should keep a good table, 'And not be like those persons mentioned by Goldsmith who spend more on chair hire than on housekeeping.'

His omniscience roused some jealousy among the younger Dons who resolved to trap him by bringing up a subject with which he would not be conversant. The conspirators met and decided that they would read up Chinese music and introduce the subject at dinner in hall. So all through dinner Chinese music was discussed. Mahaffy sat silent. Sly smiles were exchanged. At last the great man was at a loss. When finally the subject was exhausted, Mahaffy said:

'I did not like to interrupt you, gentlemen; but you will find that some of the opinions you have ventilated are those quoted by me in an article I wrote for the Encylopaedia Britannica – it must be forty years ago – as emanating from false conceptions of the nature of Chinese notations. There is nothing more likely than superficial knowledge to lead one into blunders.'

In him the knowledge and wisdom of his day resided. He aspired to the noblest things and he achieved many of them. He was an authority on learning and on matters of good taste. He was a great example to his generation. His presence had the dignity and the distinction of the XVIIIth century with none of its heaviness. He was an all-around man. His scorn was for petty things and mean men. In this he was the Most Magnificent Snob I Ever Met.

Like John Sterne, of whom he writes, 'he turned to the resources of his soul, and found in the Stoics that contentment which he ought (he confesses) to have found in the Christian faith.' In his mild and unobtrusive satire he can say, writing on the same subject: 'It is Chrysippus; it is Marcus Aurelius; it is Seneca; it is Epictetus above all who are his spiritual masters;

never once, I think, does he speak of the life and death of Jesus Christ as the source of the soul's enduring happiness. *But he never says* one word against it.' He must have smiled slightly as he penned that.

The Enigma of Dean Swift

The more we read the biographies of Dean Swift, the more we find ourselves confronted by a person who varies from an oddity to a monster, one who may hardly be included among 'the kindly race of men.' In fact, he differs outstandingly and uniquely from any character in history: all his biographers leave us with is, to say the least of it, an enigma. There is but one exception. It is a short pamphlet by that most distinguished of the Abbey Theatre's playwrights, Denis Johnson, who is also a trained lawyer. To him the solution of the jigsaw puzzle of Swift is due. His findings have been accepted by me; and it is on them that this essay is partly based.

Now it is incumbent on anyone who investigates the life of another long dead to bear in mind the fact that, in his investigations, he is apt to form his judgments by the standards of his own time. It is as hard to get away from this tendency as it is from the notion that our standards are the final word and judgment of an implacable court; whereas the fact is that century repudiates century, and civilization civilization: what is sacred in the East may be a subject for comic opera in the West. Yet there are certain standards that are universally valid. We know what Humanity is; but we must take into account the vicissitudes to which it has been subjected, the contemporary customs to which it has had to conform, and all that makes it differ from our present-day concepts. It is by making such allowances that we should judge Dean Swift.

The investigation falls under three headings or terms of reference; first, his reaction to his own times; second, his attitude towards women; third, the question of his patriotism. From these three the character of any man may be fairly deduced. When we have examined these, it will be time for a summing up to a jury of the present day.

Swift was born in No 7 Hoey's Court, Dublin, in the year 1667 in the seventh year of the reign of King Charles II. Seventy-eight years later he died in the Deanery of St Patrick's, close by the place of his birth. He was educated in Kilkenny

School, the Irish Eton of the day; and at Trinity College, Dublin.

The strange adventures of his infant years when he was kidnapped by his nurse and taken to England at the age of three, and his mother's attitude to what appears to be a convenient kidnapping, need not concern us at the moment. We are concerned with his adult years, the best part of which were spent at Moor Park, Surrey, in England, the home of Sir William Temple. Of Sir William Temple and the Temple family a reference here will not be out of place. If you look at the famous picture of the death of Sir Philip Sidney at the battle of Zutphen you will notice a man in whose arms Sir Philip is dying. This is Sir William, grandfather of the Sir William Temple of Moor Park where Swift is working. This grandfather was the first of the Temples to come to Ireland. He was a classical scholar and he became the fourth Provost of Trinity College, Dublin. His son, Sir John, was Master of the Rolls in Dublin. He wrote a history of the Irish Rebellion of 1641. He was a widower for forty years. His son, Sir William, of Moor Park, was a more prolific writer and his works were edited by Swift. This Sir William after seven years' delay on account of her family's opposition, married Dorothy Osborne by whom he had seven children of whom only one survived. To this son he made over his house at Sheen and went to reside at Moor Park where we find Swift acting as his secretary; but what is more fraught with Fate, also as tutor to a little girl, Esther, eight years old who dwelt in a pretty cottage in the grounds with her mother, a Mrs Johnson who had been Sir William's housekeeper. Her Swift instructed with an assiduity comparable (but happily incomplete) to that of Abelard toward Heloise. He called her 'Stella.'

To the man of the world Sir William Temple, Ambassador to the Hague, Swift owed his knowledge of the great moiling life beyond the quiet close of Moor Park – the world of Courts, and of courtiers and of the struggle for preference and power. He studied for six weeks in Oxford and obtained an M.A. degree. Sir William defrayed his expenses. After being shuttled to and from Ireland, at last in London he became as influential as any man who was not a member of the Court or the government. He acted as a 'lobbyist.' He was the means of obtaining offices for many a friend. Never for himself. This must not be attributed to any neglect on his part for, try as far as his pride permitted, it was not his luck to be preferred. 'A go-between' we would call him now; but in his day such activities were normal. In fact influence was the only way to preferment, that is, to obtaining office or a 'job.' That he must have been somewhat over zealous even at a time when every man as a matter of course sought influence, appears from an observation, by no means a friendly one, of Bishop Kennet who recorded in his diary for the year 1713 the swagger of Swift when he was at the height of his influence or interference in English politics, a member of a kind of inner cabinet with Harley, Harcourt and St John:

Swift came into the coffee house and had a bow from everybody but me. When I came to the ante-chamber before prayers, Dr Swift was the principal man of talk and business, and acted as minister of requests. He was soliciting the Earl of Arran to speak to his brother, the Duke of Ormonde, to get a chaplain's place established in the garrison of Hull, for Mr Fiddes, a clergyman in that neighbourhood, who had lately been in jail, and published sermons to pay fees. He was promising Mr Thorold to undertake with my Lord Treasurer that according to his petition he should obtain a salary of £200 per annum, as minister of the English church at Rotterdam. He stopped F Gwynne, Esq., going in with the red bag to the Queen, and told him aloud that he had something to say to him from my Lord Treasurer. He talked with the son of Dr Davenant to be sent abroad, and took out his pocket book and wrote down several things as memoranda to do for him. He turned to the fire and took out his gold watch and telling him the time of day, complained that it was very late. A gentleman said it was too fast. 'How can I help it,' says the Doctor, 'if the courtiers give me a watch that won't go right?' Then he instructed a young nobleman that the best poet in England was Mr Pope (a Papist) who had begun a translation of Homer into English verse, for which, he said he must have them all subscribe. 'For' said he 'the author *shall* not begin to print till I have a thousand guineas for him.' Lord Treasurer , after leaving the Queen, came through the room, beckoning Dr Swift to follow him; both went off just before prayers.

All this is rather quite in keeping with the times. What is surprising is that Bishop Kennet saw anything reprehensible in

Swift's conduct. Maybe he resented the 'swagger.' By what pretense did an obscure Irishman assume the position of 'Minister of Requests?' How came it that he made Englishmen beholden to him? Maybe the Bishop had a secret fear that, if he were to be dependent on Swift for a recommendation, he might not fare as well as the person who had been in jail.

After all, Swift did achieve something. In spite of the long delays of the court he got the First Fruits remitted. The First Fruits were a tribute to the throne of Queen Anne. Of this success he writes in that confidential diary of his which he addressed in letter form to Stella:

> As I hope to live, I despise the credit of it out of an excess of pride (significant words) and desire you will give me not the least merit when you talk of it.

The getting may have made the gift worthless in his eyes.

This 'Journal to Stella,' written in his 'little language' has been the subject of great comment. He is not the only man who has had recourse to the small or intimate language of a child. We find Sterne using it in his letters to his daughter. Swift may have employed it as a kind of cypher. There is no doubt that he intended Stella to keep this, his diary, for his future reading. We have his own words for it:

> I know it is neither wit nor diversion to tell you every day where I dine, neither do I wish it to fill my letters; but I fancy I shall, some time or another, have the curiosity of seeing some particulars how I passed my life when I was absent from M.D. this time.

M.D. was a cypher for 'my dear' when addressed solely to Stella. Sometimes it included her chaperone, Mrs Dingley, a cousin once removed of Sir William Temple. Always bearing in mind the practices of the time in which he lived (and not unmindful of our own) there is no more blame to be attached to Swift for influencing those in power than there is to Wellesley (afterwards Duke of Wellington) for soliciting his brother in India for preferment. And one hundred years after the time of Swift. The remarkable thing is that Swift, in spite of his detestation of humbug, corruption and chicane, emerges unstained from the morass of a corrupt Court, a perverted King and a corrupt Church. He was confronted with the corruption of the last when the Deanery of Derry, the richest plum in the

Irish Church, was sold over his head by the man, Bush, who had already intrigued him out of the secretary-ship to Lord Berkeley, to the highest bidder. The highest bidder was Dr Theophilus Bolton who, in spite of his Christian name, or, perhaps, because of it, paid one thousand pounds for the love of God. So much for practices of the times in which he lived.

Now let us turn to Swift's relationship with women. In spite of the precursor of Freud, Kraft-Ebing, who pronounced on reading 'The Diary to Stella,' that Swift was 'sexually anaesthetic,' we have convincing evidence to the contrary. Here are two of his letters concerning liaisons in his youth:

> This woman, my mistress with a pox, left one daughter, Anne by name. This Anne, for it must be she, about seven years ago writ me from London to tell me she was the daughter of Betty Jones, for that was my mistresses name.

That is one on his own avowal; but –

> I could remember twenty women in my life to whom I have behaved myself in just the same way; and I profess without any other design than that of entertaining myself when I am very idle or when something goes amiss in my affairs. This I have always done as a man of the world when I had no design for anything grave in it, and what I thought at worst a harmless impertinence. But whenever I begin to take sober resolutions, or, as now, to think of entering the Church, I never found it would be hard to put off this kind of folly at the porch.

This brings to mind a conversation I had years ago with another famous divine, who, like Swift, was an alumnus of Trinity College: 'My dear fellow, I have had sixty-five love affairs. I never regretted one of them, never! But' – with a twinkle – 'they were all before I was ordained.'

Here is another letter written to a Miss Waring whom he sued vehemently and called her his Varina after his fashion, only to be refused by her. When afterwards she confessed her willingness to marry him, what she got by way of a missive was this. After telling her that he would overlook her shortcomings in good looks and income, he proceeded –

> Have you such an inclination to my person and humour as to comply with my desires and way of living, and endeavour to

make us both as happy as you can? Will you be ready to engage in those methods I shall direct for the improvement of your mind, so as to make us entertaining company for each other without being miserable when we are neither visiting or being visited? Can you bend your love and esteem and indifference to others in the same way as I do mine?

This letter shows him most disadvantageously. Since we do not know what went to its making, judgment must be reserved; but one thing is plain; that is that no one who had any spirit could accept the positon of the household drudge which was at the time apparently Swift's requirement of a wife.

Contrast it with the childish tenderness of his love for Stella. Now we come to another Esther. She is Esther Vanhomrigh, daughter of a Lord Mayor of Dublin. She herself was given the freedom of that city. We find her living with her mother in London at the time that Swift was at the height of his power. He was familiar with the family; and he used their home to change his wig and gown. Very often he dined there. Esther, soon to become 'Vanessa,' was an impulsive, generous and passionate young woman. She was interested in books and was superior in intelligence to the young bloods of London who frequented the coffee houses and the theatres. Her admiration of Swift and her flattery could not long be resisted by a heart that was hungering for admiration. She is never mentioned directly in his Journal to Stella.

The condition of the native population of Ireland of Swift's day is unspeakable. Its starving savages in the most fertile land in Europe constitute a blot on the humanity of England that is indelible. For cold callousness she can be unexcelled. 'Quite certainly,' said the great Bishop, George Berkeley, 'there is nowhere so beggarly, wretched and destitute a people as the Irish.'

There is not space to go into the horrid details of a prolonged national crime that exceeded the swifter attempts at genocide of our day. The capacity of England's agents for misgoverning is appalling. In one thing they outdo the excesses of any tyranny: their persecutions are directed against colonists of their own flesh and blood. It was this injustice, an injustice directed against the little Protestant colony in Ireland, and not that against the mere Irish, that filled Swift's breast with the *saeva indignatio* against oppression. It could but include, whether he intended it or not, the wrongs of the natives in common with the community of which he was a member.

Swift could exaggerate when occasion rose. He exalted his mother's-pedigree from that of a butcher's daughter to a descendant of a family that had fought against the Normans. If Erick was a Norse name there were Norsemen in England before the Normans but there is no evidence that they fought at Hastings. He made his mother a relative of Sir William Temple's wife. This to account for the favors he received from Sir William; but it may be taken as a presumption that he knew he had something to explain.

He was unfair concerning the value of Woods' haifpence; he used exaggeration to help argument. Most of the fury in Ireland rose not against the token value of the coins as against the attempt of the King to make the Irish pay for the keep of his German mistress.

His proposal, no matter what motives instigated it, for 'The Universal Use of Irish Manufacture' makes him the father of Sinn Fein (ourselves alone). Anent this service of Swift to the Irish, listen to Dr Johnson who cannot be regarded altogether as a friendly commentator:

> He taught them first to know their own interest; their weight and strength, and gave them spirit to assert that equality with their fellow subjects, to which ever since they have been making vigorous advances, and to claim those rights which they have at last established.

Here the glimpses at Swift's reaction to the times in which he lived; his attitude towards women and his patriotism, end. Now let us turn to the talk about him which still goes on in Dublin.

I had been photographing a colored bust of Swift bewigged, which is set in a niche above a tavern in Werburgh Street at the corner of Hoey's Court, now a walled-up and dismantled cul de sac, when I decided to lunch at the lavish Dolphin where they serve the best lunch in Dublin. There it was my good luck to find two eminent men of letters. One was Denis Johnson, best of the Abbey Theatre dramatists who survive and the latest authority on the origin of Swift. The other was Lynn Doyle, the poet and the sophisticated writer of many a simple story.

Our talk was a causerie covering many aspects and many incidents of the life of the Dean. 'I have always regarded him as a second-rate writer,' said Lynn Doyle. I could not be surprised at that because I knew well how exigent the speaker's ideas of great writing were; and I had the conflicting opinions of Swift's commentators in mind. For instance Hume who said, 'His style contains no harmony, no eloquence, no ornament and not much correctness.' Mackintosh called it, 'Proper, pure, precise, perspicacious, significant, nervous.' And I remembered my friend Dr Yelverton Tyrrell, Professor of Greek in Trinity College, telling me how at a dinner he sat next to Carlyle and took the opportunity of asking him whom he considered the best prose writer in the English language. The sage answered without hesitation, 'Swift, for his perfect lucidity.' With these three in mind I asked Lynn Doyle how he came to such a conclusion. 'Swift never wrote out of his subconscious,' was the answer. To that I had to concede. Had not Dryden testified to it when he said, 'Cousin Swift, you will never be a poet' Poetry, in spite of his readiness in rhyme and his multitudinous verses, was as far away from Swift as from another great Dublin intellect and master of clear prose, George Bernard Shaw. To neither of them had the vision beautiful been vouchsafed. Think of Shakespeare, Blake, Tennyson, Yeats. I would not have dragged them into such a comparison were it not for others' pretensions to the poetic leaf.

Denis Johnson was saying, 'The Black Book of the King's Inns would repay anyone interested in research of the period. It has not yet been edited. In it we can see the handwriting of the Jonathan Swift who was reputedly the father of the famous Jonathan. Sometimes it is blotted and blurred. The writer was evidently drunk when he wrote. Sometimes there was no entry. He did not write at all.'

I said, 'This was the man on whom Sir John Temple wished his mistress, Abagail Erick, when he thought that it was time to make provision for her.'

'He was about sixty-six,' Denis Johnson continued, still referring to Abagail's husband. 'He disappears from the picture. The entries cease in November 1666. He died probably during the winter or the spring of 1667. On the last day of the November following, his widow gave birth to a child – ten or eleven months later.'

I thought of how long Jonathan the Elder may have been ailing before his death. I thought of the consolation his widow got when she turned for comfort to Sir John Temple, her old protector. Enough to make her the mother of his child who was christened Jonathan to add verisimilitude. But Vanessa was the woman of whom I wanted information. I got it. She followed Swift to Ireland in 1715 despite his earnest attempts to dissuade her. She had property in what is now Celbridge Abbey. It was called Marlay Abbey in those days. We do not have to consult Walpole who was an enemy of Swift to sense a liaison between the passionate, generous Vanessa and the man who bred true to the Temples. In Dublin of the scandals it is not to be assumed that there was not some talk of Swift's doubtful parentage, The gossips overshot the mark by suggesting that he was a son of Sir William Temple and, therefore, a half-brother to Stella. The Revolution of 1689 and the Battle of the Boyne were distractions enough to keep the gossips busy with other themes. As Denis Johnson said, 'A new generation had forgotten the old Master of the Rolls and connected Swift with the son instead of with the father.'

But the jigsaw puzzle is solved. Every piece fits in if you realize that Swift was the half-brother of Sir William Temple. It makes him the uncle of little 'Stella' Johnson, and not the half-brother. But the relationship is enough to put marriage out of the question. The common law of England, not to mention Church Law, made such a relationship as marriage between an uncle and a niece incestuous. Vanessa was living in Ireland for nine years. She could stand her equivocal position no longer. She wrote to Stella. Swift got the letter. He took horse to Marlay Abbey cold with fury. He threw her letter at Vanessa. The warm heart broke. It was the end of her and that affair.

As for Stella, the happy, the heroic, the witty and the devoted, biographers make her out to be the victim of Swift's sexual anaesthesia. She was his niece. Once that was revealed to her all was clear. She could have chosen anyone; but to her devotion to her old tutor she made a sacrifice which has been the cause of both mystery and scandal. Was there ever a dilemma more acute than Swift's? He could not marry Vanessa who had claims on him sufficient to impel her to follow him to Ireland, without confessing his blood relationship with Stella, a secret not altogether his to divulge; nor could he marry Vanessa without putting Stella, if he kept the secret, in the unjust and invidious position of a discarded mistress. Is it any wonder that as Archbishop Narcissus King said mysteriously to Dr Delaney who had seen the Dean rush out distractedly, 'You have just seen the most unhappy man on earth; but on the subject of his wretchedness you must never ask a question'?

When did Swift know of his illegitimacy? Surely when he began to regard himself as an Englishman. The fact that he condemned Ireland is enough to make us realize that he considered himself to be of a different breed.

How are we to make him human and understandable unless we grant that he was the victim of an unrightable wrong, and that he knew it? The wrong of his birth which he never confessed worked inwardly and filled him with innate dissatisfaction. He knew the magnitude of a power that unobtrusively ruled England for two years, and he knew that he could never lay claim to an origin which could make that intellectual superiority not seem upstart, extraordinary and impertinent. To a mind of such sensitivity as Swift's, illegitimacy was the greatest wrong that could be inflicted on him. It came like the Nemesis of a Greek tragedy, an unexplainable, undeserved injustice. Is it any wonder that injustice was the subject of his frenzy and his indignation? To this was added an inevitable corollary of another illegitimacy, the one disabling him from marrying where his heart lay. He was sentenced to secrecy, celibacy and, as he imagined, contempt in high places.

Charges against his integrity as a divine, as a politician and a lover fade into trifles when confronted with the integrity of his life. The necessity for concealment hid even his pity, 'demonic pity' Denis Johnson called it, for the mortal race of men. To conceal his kindness, his self-sacrifice and his charity, he had to assume the manner of abruptness and the mask of the cynic. All the good he did was as indirect as his parentage. Scourging the corruption of the times he lived in, he condemned forever all corruption, and denouncing more fiercely than any man has done before or since the injustice to the country to which Fate condemned him, he became the hierophant of human liberty.

Let him be judged first by his detractors. Envy and blindness distracted three of them. Professional maliciousness invalidates Jeffrey. Dr Johnson did his best to be fair. But Thackeray and Macauley can make no allowances for Nature had deprived them of the understanding required to penetrate into the fastnesses held by such a haughty castellan. They were blinded by their political grudges.

There is another and an infallible way of judging a man. For this I am indebted to the poet, James Stephens: 'How many men loved him?' That is the test. Bolingbroke who lived in life-long intimacy with Swift wrote, 'I love you for a thousand things.' Even Vanessa, discarded and heart-broken, acknowledges, 'I know your good nature is such that you cannot see any human creature miserable without being sensibly touched.'

Twice he loaned his all and lost it to friends. In Ireland where he had to be disguised and more guarded, the penetration of the common wretches saw behind his mask. It is over two hundred years since his death, and, regardless of misunderstanding, he is still spoken of as a patriot who won love and admiration in spite of himself from a populace who were incapable of appreciating any gifts but those of the heart.

The Bullyns in Ireland

Offaly is one of the midmost counties. The land is fertile and well-watered. I felt that there must be castles in it. Now when a castle is mentioned in Ireland the mind calls up a fortified ruin in more or less decay. Castles are all that remain in the land to show to what stormy times and devastations it has been subjected; they were built when there was no living without them: men had either to live in a strong castle or in a lowly cottage out of sight, in order to survive. They who lived in cottages did not, as a rule, contribute to history. Those who lived in castles did, either as victors or victims; and they got into the news which was chiefly scandal in the days of Queen Elizabeth or, rather especially, of her father, Henry VIII.

I was looking up the local history when I came across the phrase, 'Maw 'Coghlan of the Fair Castles.' I realized that he lived in the vicinity three hundred years ago. 'Surely,' I said to myself, 'he must have had remarkable fortresses, else he would not have earned such a title at a time when anyone who counted lived in a guarded home.' Here was I within a few miles of his dominions. It was time to stop reading about them and start to search for the Fair Castles for myself.

Now all my life I have been taken by lovely and romantic things. There was a time when I used to collect lakes even if they were hardly bigger than large ponds. Then I collected little waterfalls. And there was a time when I used to go stalking castles. Do not think me mad if I use the word 'stalking.' Anyone who has sighted a castle suddenly and then, just as suddenly, lost it in a fold of the hills, will know what I mean. You see it now; and then you lose it because a tangle of briar intervenes. When you emerge it is still lost until you catch sight of it again from a clearing on a rising field; as soon as you leave the high ground it is gone again; and, sometimes, when you are closest to it, it is hardest to find. Old castles are not to be come upon by the roadside, but in far fields or by the sides of rivers or lakes or the strand of the sea. Those that stood by a highway were, as likely as not, pulled down to make road metal by native contractors who had not yet risen to an appreciation of their country's history.

Luckily I was staying with a friend to whom such things as old castles and landmarks were dear. 'Yes,' he said, 'I know a goodly castle not far from Shinrone. I will bring round the Buick and off we will go.'

We passed through a countryside full of great trees with horizontal boughs that sprung low down, a sign that the land from which they rose was rich though, here and there, reeds showed in the middle of fields, proofs that the land was in need of drainage. There were not wanting signs that a drainage scheme was in progress; mechanical shovels rose along the river bank, and along the river bank we went, for by it stood Clonoony, the castle of our quest. We came to the little village of Cloghan. We had gone past it hardly a mile when we were under the castle walls. It was surrounded by a containing wall, for in the days it was built, the flocks and herds had to be sheltered before the fight began. We got out and found that we had to stand back across the road to see to the top of its dungeon tower. This, like the outer fortifications, was crenellated, that is, provided with battlements, which is un-usual because in most castles the top wall is breast high. It suggested something built after the Waverley novels appeared, for then every man who lived in a castle had his walls crenellated and this modern feudalism did not stop at castles. I have seen a battlemented public house.

Nevertheless, Clonoony castle was the real thing. It is even still in fairly good preservation despite the ignorance and apathy of the Irish people. It dates back to before the reign of Henry VIII to the time when its builder, The Maw 'Coghlan flourished. Henry VIII's reign began in 1509. In that year in Ireland, the Four Masters tell us, in Devlin, not far from Clonoony, a great contest arose between the tribe of Fergal McCoghlan and the tribe of Donal in which James McCoghlan, prior of Gallen, and heir presumptive of Devlin Eathra, was killed by the shot of a ball from the castle of Cluan Damchna (Clonoony). This shows that the place was the residence of the heir apparent to the princes of the district – for 'cluan' means in Gaelic a plain; and 'damchna' means the successor or one eligible to become successor to the prince.

The 'shot of a ball' may seem a curious expression; but it is one full of interest for it is used to differentiate between the

67

shot of an arrow or of a quarrel from a crossbow. It does not occur until forearms were imported into Ireland. They came – is it surprising – from Germany. The first muskets to be seen in Dublin came in from that country in the year 1498. And the garrison of Clonoony lost no time in acquiring the most modern of 'secret' weapons.

Through a gate in the outer wall we entered. A large courtyard opened out before us. One side was bordered by the river Brosna, a small and fordable stream. Two sides were closed by the containing wall. From the fourth rose the castle, one side of which was based on the living rock.

Up the winding stairs we went; but we could not climb more than two stories for the steps had fallen away. On the steps that were still intact we noticed rings of metal set in lead in each step a few inches from the sides. They looked like iron nails about three inches long which had been bent back so as not to pierce the feet of those who visited the ruin and climbed its stair. I have been in many castles; but I never saw their like before. Through a shot window glimpses of the surrounding country could be caught; but the view was not satisfactory: shot windows are not made for scenery; as we could not reach the top, what the prospect looked like from that height we could not tell; but, undoubtedly the fair champaign was unrolled under a sun that threw great shadows of cloud across its expanse. Over the stream the remains of another castle could be seen. At least so I was told; but I did not notice any remains. I was also told that there was an underground passage from Clonoony to the castle over the river – the voice of the people no doubt; for countrymen love underground passages and all mysterious subterranean things. That one existed I do not hesitate to believe. There is one from Melrose castle in Scotland to the fort that stands beyond the brook; but there is nothing mystical about it. In practical Scotland the purpose of such a passage was as simple as it was economic; it was tunnelled so that one garrison could defend two castles if they were attacked in turn.

We had come out to the spacious yard or garth when my friend drew my attention to a large flat stone about eight feet by four and a foot thick which was lying in the middle of the courtyard. It had evidently been used as a seat where rustics played cards or children climbed. The middle of it was worn. It had been recently chipped.

The history of this stone is somewhat remarkable. At the beginning of the last century some labourers were sent to collect building material for the barracks which were to be erected near by; and for the canal locks near the castle – we can well wonder how the castle was left. They began about 100 yards from the castle. They discovered a hollow in the limestone rock in which was a heap of stones. When this heap was taken away, it was seen that it had been placed there to hide something buried beneath. At a depth of twelve feet they uncovered the slab. On removing this there appeared a kind of coffin or sarcophagus cut in the solid rock. It contained the skeletons of two persons. When the slab was brought into the light an inscription then perfectly legible was found. This is the slab I have described; and, though the inscription is much worn now and rendered indecipherable by exposure, it is recorded that it read in letters incised on its face:

> Here under leys Elizabeth and Mary Bullyn daughters of Thomas Bullyn son of George Bullyn the son of George Bullyn Viscount Rochford son of Sir Thomas Bullyn Erle of Ormonde and Wiltshire.

All I could read was the last line or two. In the 2nd last line the name *Bullyn* was spelt with only one 'l,' though there was space left for a second 'l' which was never incised.

Elizabeth and Mary Bullyn (for it was the skeletons of these ladies that occupied the tomb) were no less than second cousins of Queen Elizabeth. Their grandfather was cousin-german of Anne Bullyn, the famous and unfortunate consort of King Henry VIII. Now to go back a little in the history the epitaph gives us, the George Rochford whose grandchildren the ladies were, was Viscount Rochford, Anne Bullyn's brother. The ladies, his grandchildren, came to Ireland from Chester in the latter part of the seventeenth century. and settled near Shinrone. Let us not make the mistake, however tempting, into which archaeologists very often fall and say that, because their skeletons were found near a place, their owners must have inhabited it when living. But it has been pointed out that if you were a person of consequence, you had to live in a castle and, though the place in which the skeletons were found may have been a part of the old cemetery of Clonoony, it does not necessarily follow that Elizabeth and Mary lived in the castle of Clonoony. But where else was there for them to live? Maw

'Coghlan had many 'fair castles.' There must have been one close to Clonoony because the underground tunnel to it is said to exist. One of these castles or the castle of Clonoony may have been rented from the Maw 'Coghlan or taken over from one of his tribes. The interesting fact is that we find the Bullyns in Ireland shortly after the reign of Henry VIII. What happened?

We know that the Erle of Wiltshire, that is the original and presumably the lawful possessor of the title, was forced to give it up in favor of George Bullyn, the brother of Queen Anne Bullyn. By as capricious an act of Henry's may not the family of Bullyn have been distrained after the beheading of the Queen? Ireland was a place – strange as it may sound – of refuge in those days. It was also a place of banishment. Obviously, dispossessed persons lost caste and with it all interest in the old environment. What the reason may have been for their presence in the country, disaffected as it was to Henry and his works, there is not the slightest doubt that, after the murder of Queen Anne Bullyn, a considerable time after it though it was, the Bullyn family came to Ireland about 1680 and we find the skeletons of two of the unmarried ladies of that family interred within a hundred yards of Clonoony castle, within its grounds in fact. To pursue the story further, the sister of Elizabeth and Mary, sister Anne, married, in spite of her unpropitious name, Sir Robert Newcomen and through him several Irish families can claim cousinship with Anne Bullyn's daughter, Queen Elizabeth.

The subject is one to awaken the curiosity of historians. What brought the father of these ladies, Elizabeth and Mary, to Ireland? Did he come to take part in the devastations Queen Elizabeth wrought there when her favorite, The Earl of Essex, wasted his time campaigning against separate fortresses and captains instead of facing that destroyer of English armies, the great O'Neill? That on the face of it is most unlikely. Nor is there anyone by the name of Bullyn in a position of command suitable to a member of a family which gave a Queen to the throne of England. What was Thomas Bullyn doing in this out of the way place? Evidently he lived here, and here his family grew up and were married and peacefully interred. What is the answer? The answer is that the Irishry welcomed an English refugee as they do to the present day. Anyone who suffered as the Bullyn family did must have received a hearty and an

70

understanding welcome in a land that suffered so much under Elizabeth that only three houses were built throughout the country during her long reign; and one of them was what some of the autochthonti still regard as a proselytizing institution.

Did a descendant of him of The Fair Castles provide the Bullyns with a home out of his abundance? Things must have grown quiet since 1545 when 'Edmond Fahy encamped before the castle of Fadan one of the Fair Castles, for the space of eight days, and Cormac Maw 'Coghlan who was in the castle, was compelled to give him hostages after which he and Edmond made a gossipship with each other.' Even though that *gossipship* must have been somewhat terse and maybe monosyllabic, I would have loved to have listened in on it.

They chose the place of their exile well. The territory of The Maw 'Coghlan was a little principality. He coined his own money and made his own laws; and very probably extended a protecting hand to the newcomers. They must have lived in amity with their neighbors and amid a civilization that was if anything more civil than that which had accepted the act of beheading a woman, however unpopular, with complacency. The portraits of Elizabeth and Mary are said to be in the possession of the present Lord Rosse. What more proof is required to show that there was at one time a long spell of peace and culture around the castle of Clonoony?

Let Us Now Praise Famous Men

Nowadays there seems to be a formula for vilifying the great, a formula that takes what Dean Swift calls a *mean* man to apply. It begins by the critic or biographer, as the case may be, taking you into his confidence and thereby elevating himself by implying that you and he are too much men of the world to be fooled by hero worship. Insensibly you come to share his opinion that great men are merely men whom you and he could emulate if you cared to compete. He prefers however to remain superior in his own superior way. To prove his superiority he gathers up every unfortunate or unedifying detail of his victim's childhood and adolescence. If possible some report of his nurse or his schoolmaster; then some remark of his wife, or, more convincing, of his mistress if he had one. If he had not, that can be turned into a shortcoming. The aim is to give trivialities more prominence than achievements.

If in some cases, such as that of Lord Nelson whose philandering has endeared him to the great heart of England, this scheme will not succeed, then some other no less contemptible trick may be employed to drag him down so that his critic or biographer goes up. It might be proved that he lived at a time when the natural expansion of the nation made achievement easy, as easy as it was during the spacious days of Queen Elizabeth. If this fails then there is the treatment by silence. This may be the reason that we hear so little about the achievements of Sir Walter Raleigh. True, he is mentioned now and again but he is presented more as the showman who laid his cloak under the feet of a favour-bestowing Queen than as the great innovator of the naval strategy of his day, the colonizer of India and America, the developer of Virginia and the believer in its great future, the bringer of the gold of Guiana; of the potato, quinine, and tobacco to Europe; the soldier-sailor-saviour of his country. He is a supreme example of the injustice of debunkers, for Raleigh fell a victim to a wolfish pact of the detractors of his time who were in the pay of the enemy, men whose howls of envy eventually sent him to the scaffold.

Wordsworth, Wellington and Columbus among many have been the subjects of modern 'research.' Their biographers have discovered that Wordsworth and Columbus were the fathers of illegitimate children. We are told that Columbus might have been canonized but for this by men who are ignorant of the fact that such an encumbrance was no obstacle to the honours of the altar in St Augustine's case. Milton who, unfortunately for the biographer of his wife, had not the distinction of profligacy, has his domesticity turned against him. He becomes an impossible husband, an exacting father, and a household bully, anything but 'the third amongst the sons of light' and the most mellifluous of the English poets. Wellington who 'never lost an English gun' is distinguished for his answer to a blackmailer – 'Publish and be damned.'

What is the reason for this emphasis on detraction? It is twofold. It comes from the time in which we live and its effect on some of the people in it. Ours is an age of disruptions which cast their shadows before them in literature. The upheaval which ultimately followed the distortions of Hegelism can be seen in the revolt against form and against literature itself in the work of Arthur Rimbaud and, later, in the James Joyce who began by modelling himself on Rimbaud. Classical forms and scholasticism were smashed to pieces, and, just as the ignoramuses of the Middle Ages made amulets out of the texts of Virgil, the fragments are worshipped and venerated by those who are apparently incapable of appreciating the design of the originals.

The second of the twofold causes that make greatness and beauty intolerable to mean men is in the individual.

To discover the cause for this spate of detraction, we must turn the tables on the detractors and delve into the history of their childhood. Psychiatrists tell us that those who grow up to hate have been misunderstood in their childhood and deprived of parental sympathy and love. They have been punished and corrected until feelings of rage and fear followed by guilt are engendered, feelings which fuse into hatred as the child grows up. He hates his parents; and, by the time he is an adult, he hates all authoritative persons because they have become for him parent images. 'Greatness' he hates because by that his character has become blighted. Thus the blighted becomes the blighter. This may be one way of explaining the present remarkable and unremitting attempts to decry and to vilify men who have spent great souls in ennobling the human race. By corollary it may explain the inflated reputations that have been gained by unworthy men.

There can be playful 'debunkings' which are harmless because they are amusing, good-humoured, perceptive and the reverse of malign. Here is one by a man who knew and could repeat every lyric of importance in the language, and some that were of no importance. He was commenting on Walter Landor's assertion:

I fought with none for none was worth my strife,
Nature I loved, and, after Nature, Art.
I warmed both hands before the fire of Life.
It sinks, and I am ready to depart.

'If you want to hear the truth,' was the comment, 'he fought with everyone, including his wife, whom, on their honeymoon, he threw out of the window on to a bed of Neapolitan violets. Nature he loved and, after Nature, Art. Yet anyone could sell him an oleograph for an old master. He warmed both hands before the fire of Life whereas he lived in self-imposed seclusion in Florence. He is ready to depart! He hesitated and hung on for eighty-nine years.'

An idea can be as inspiring as spring, or deadlier than an atomic bomb and radio-active for generations. In the Middle Ages, for instance, the idea of the Virgin Mother was central and dynamic. From this hyperdulia arose beauty in the arts and sainthood in society. Nowadays many minds are centred on moulds and nuclear energy; penicillin and ethereal disruption and disruptive ideas that would blast beauty and grandeur from the face of the earth.

I think it is high time that we turned to praise of famous men. For Humanity was never in greater need of magnanimous ideas and noble examples. Men who spread civilization or saved it; men who array Truth in the noblest forms of human speech; men who magnify men's souls until they transcend the bounds of Time – these are the bastions of Man's spirit and the exponents of his worth.

So much the rather let us praise famous men. Let us praise them if for no other but the selfish reason that the act of praise

74

exalts the praiser above pettiness and soul-scald, and draws him closer to the object of his laudation.

Let us praise famous men if only to save ourselves from the cynical sophistication of our time, from the venom of little men whose parents did not love them.

INTIMATIONS

Intimations

Sounds inaudible to others, like sweet voices in a dream

It needs silence without and stillness within to overhear the heavenly messages; the practical mind must be diverted and the ears and eyes thrown out of focus on mundane affairs before we can catch the far-off converse of the Immortals, for they are neither seen nor heard by earthly organs, but perceived only by that within us which is like to them.

This is no new discovery. It has been known from time out of mind. It is what the poets and prophets tell us. It is behind all spiritual religion. It is the mystery that lies deep within the liturgies. It is the means by which a man becomes a saint or a poet. Without it nothing is authentically divine. Though the adepts can transmit it, everyone must experience it for himself. There must be contemplation before there can be inspiration.

Because a man may speak about this only for himself, I can only tell how and where I lie, 'waiting for the spark from Heaven to fall,' for there are certain places more favorable for this experience than others. Obviously in the hustling and roaring street where a man's wits have all they can do to steer him safely through the traffic, it is unlikely that he will hear the untranslatable speech or feel the presence of the divine. Mountains, brooks and dingles, through the foliage of which you can see the sky, are more likely to be haunted.

There is a brook in leafy Vermont by which I love to lie for hours to gaze at that mixture of water and light, aware that I am sib to the dewdrop and the rainbow. This may seem to contradict what has been said about the need for silence; but it is not a great contradiction, for the sound of a brook has never altered any more than the silent voice of inspiration; the same sound has been heard by Homer as by Shakespeare and Coleridge. It does not sing in any human tongue yet its language is understood by all. It is that water which Pindar called 'best of all,' the very speech of inspiration. Water, first of singers, was 'the skyborn brook.'

Thus it is no distraction, for it sings in the language of the skies, and that is the only language that has a message for us all. While listening to it you cease to hear it, but catch instead sounds inaudible to others, like sweet voices in a dream. A man is lucky if he can record this music, for it fades before it can be taken down. Its rhythm is all that I can hope to hear. This experience is not mine only, nor this belief.

I saw the other day in a window a statue of a beautiful youth with a bowed head and a pointed finger. From his left shoulder hung the chlamys, or short Greek cloak. His feet were buskined. His eyes were on the ground. It was a copy of the statue of 'The Listener'; but the pose was not one of attention such as that we might give to the movements of an enemy. It was one of rapture; he was listening and, hearing, was transfigured in beauty. The full title of the statue was 'Dionysus listening to Echo.' I said to myself, 'There is the answer to all who say that what we listen to is only an echo of ourselves.'

Very well, then. But what if that which is in ourselves is a memory of the great poetry of all time, or the heroic deeds of men? Of necessity it must be but an echo, for the diapason would be too great to bear, certainly too great to be expressed. For this reason inspiration is neither complete nor continuous.

There is another thought which is inspiring: it is that this inspiration or enthusiasm can be transmitted from man to man, to the novice from the adept. And there are many men and women who can transmit it. In some cases their presence is enough. Others can transmit it by example or the spoken word. They have in them something of the Immortals' bodily shape or mighty mind. Love and reverence are needed before we can receive what they have to give, just as silence and stillness are needed if the inspiration is to come from within.

I do not know whether the impulse I get from a natural object is stronger than the emotion with which I hail a friend. I confess that I shouted with joy last spring, when, in a little wood in Maryland, I came upon a tree all white with bloom in the middle of the wood's fresh green. There was no one there to hear me. Had there been, I might have been taken away to be psychoanalyzed by one of those maddening mechanics who dissect the mind as if it were a mere material thing. From them is the vision withheld. I wonder to what they would attribute the joy I felt when I saw beside the wood a mist of light blue flowers lying like a little lake of azure in a yellow field. I know how I feel when I meet a godlike person – he causes the heart to sing. I know, too, whether it be an 'impulse from a vernal wood' or the presence of a magnanimous soul; the effect is one and the same thing. It is the divine speaking directly and, perhaps, in the only way it ever does to man.

And the effect of these intimations is ecstasy, an extension of oneself to become merged in divinity. Saints, poets and certain philosophers have experienced it. Plotinus called it 'achieving the term.' Porphyry tells us, speaking of Plotinus: 'The Master achieved the term three times. I, Porphyry, but once.' It comes rarely in rare lives; to the generality, never. I knew a great poet who was overwhelmed by this bliss but once in his life. He felt blessed and able to bless. The mood lasted but twenty minutes; but those minutes were worth his earthly life span, for they were more than intimations. They were more than assurances. They were the actual experience of immortality.

Manners Maketh Man

These words are engraved over the gate of New College, Oxford; and over the entrance to Winchester College where those Civil Servants who are the backbone of the English Government are trained. It matters not to them what governments come or go, they are permanent. They write the speeches for Conservative, Liberal or Labor Governments and the Speech from the Throne with complete detachment. Governments come and go; but they go on, if not forever, for a lifetime of silent service. They receive a knighthood when they retire, and they spend their remaining days in the best Conservative clubs where, by example, they set the mysterious code of what is done and what is not done. In a word, they are the exponents of good manners. Manners made them. It is their duty to maintain the makings of men: and to set the fashion of behavior.

Manners are wonderful in their own way for, no matter how poor a creature the exponent of them may be, if he sticks to the code of good manners, he will pass through life respected. He will come very near to having what amounts to a personality of his own.

Now what does the code ordain? It ordains that a man must have honor, self-restraint and, above all, a consideration for the feelings of others. 'Good manners,' said Dean Swift, 'is the art of making those people easy with whom we converse.' And someone else has said that a gentleman is he who has respect for the feelings of others. From this it would appear that manners maketh gentlemen. How can it be otherwise if one complies with the conventions set out above?

No one should have to consult a dictionary to find out what manners are; but it is interesting nevertheless to read that the word 'manners' is derived from the Latin, *manus*, which means the hand; and from that it comes by some sort of punning to mean the way a person handles, first of all himself; and then whatever situation he finds himself in.

To a great extent good manners are the outcome of good upbringing.

Education helps to develop character, to educe it, not to suppress it. Good manners develop with the growth of character.

So far, we have looked upon manners as being all that are required to make a man; but what about those great souls who are already pre-eminent in their own right? What of the men who already have character? Men whose spell still lives on and is felt as a stimulus or a deterrent?

If empty men can be made significant as was the late Lord Curzon merely by a grand manner, what of men great in their own right?

Julius Caesar was said to have had the most persuasive way with him and a personal charm which was nothing short of magnetism. He was loved by men and women and by his armies; and hated by the meanest people of his time. This in itself was a distinction. And are we not in the presence of a magnificent figure when we read about Pompey the Great, with his 'curtesie in conversation so that there was never man that requested anything with less ill will than he, nor that more willingly did pleasure unto any man when he was requested, for he gave without disdain and took with great handsomeness'?

'Great handsomeness!' What a description that is! In it all that manners mean is contained. This is where a great soul is communicating itself.

Now the question arises: Can good manners be attained? The answer is: Most certainly. I have already spoken of Lord Curzon who was a mannikin of manners. They say that he was ruined by a couplet written about him by some jiber at Oxford,

'I am George Nathaniel Curzon
And a most superior person.'

but, evidently, his attitudinizing must have been already there else he would not have brought the rhyme on himself. Yet, in spite of all, he made quite a name as an ambassador, and no doubt he owed all to the permanent Civil Servants who cannot go wrong. Both were lapped in 'good form.' If, as in Curzon's case, good manners can be acquired so that they make a personality, it stands to reason that they can alter a person's for the better. I have seen quite unprepossessing women, for example, who were so charming that not only was their lack of good looks set off; but they became almost an attraction. This was due to some extent to vivacity, but more to their power of 'making those people easy' with whom they conversed. It is not necessary to go to a school of acting to achieve this. All that is needed is a tolerance for others and an absorbing interest in things, in life: – vivacity and interest in others. Above all, there must be poise. It is hard to imagine a flighty person possessing the power of putting others at their ease seeing that the flighty person is not at ease at all. But it quite easy to imagine or to recall many instances of ugly people with charm and beautiful ways of handling situations. Intelligence is necessary, for without intelligence men cannot impress by their opinion or interest us by their experience. Wit in a woman is irresistible. 'Manner more than gold is the adornment of a woman' (Menander). Education is an indispensable requirement. I have met highly learned and specialized minds utterly failing to communicate their knowledge because of a blunder in pronunciation or grammar. Why this should prove an obstacle to social intercourse, I think I can tell. It arises from an association of ideas inseparable in the mind, an association of elementary schooling with advanced learning which, in the case of some childish error, invalidates everything else. A man can be a profound scientist and yet totally unfitted for polite society. He has no method by which he can 'handle' the situation. He has no manners.

Mrs Bernard Shaw was fully cognizant of this when she declared in her will that,

> 'I have had many opportunities of observing the extent to which the most highly instructed and capable persons have their efficiency defeated and their influence limited for the want of any organized instruction and training for personal contacts whether with individuals or with popular audiences, without which their knowledge is incommunicable.'

So she left her money to teach Irishmen manners, not all of them, but those who, 'in spite of great attainments, lacked address.' She did not allude to her husband. Mrs Bernard Shaw said that, not I; yet I had better make my peace with Irishmen who might want to know why I brought the subject up, by first using an Englishman as an example of the deterrent effect of ignorance of grammar on his influence. I knew a very competent English artist who was quite unfitted to take the place his talents deserved in society because of his lack of primary education.

"Ow can 'e meet me without I being there?' Why should this and a Cockney accent be enough to invalidate a man? The reason or, rather, the cause is that we expect a man whose brain is capable of great things to be able to master the rudiments of polite speech and to familiarize himself with the usages of society. It comes to this then: bad grammar is bad manners.

I knew an outstanding genius who loved this country and came to visit it frequently; but he pained the listener now and again by a mispronounced word or a solecism. When a slight mistake was coupled with his great achievement in letters, the effect was floundering. He was one of those whom Mrs Shaw included in her will.

If comparatively humble people like artists and literary men suffer from the lack of manners what are we to think of those in high places who have none? I know one statesman or politician (latterly they tend to merge) who, being totally devoid of regard for the feelings of others, is little better than a bully and a boor. He is so full of himself that he has no room for anything else. Perhaps it is just as well because his own judgments are infallibly wrong.

Two men I knew whose manners were remarkable in a society where all were distinguished. The late Lord Middleton, who invented the flat-topped cap which has become universal in all armies, and the late Duke of Connaught. These men could put you at your ease and send you away with the impression that it really mattered to them what you said.

It may not be an infringement of good manners to be too brainy but ostentatious opinion or learning is an anathema. The father of Matthew Arnold must have felt this when he established the 'old school tie' and erred in the opposite direction. He went too far when he tried to substitute conformity to code for brains, or, perhaps I should say, originality, which is still bad form in the great schools and at the universities of England. Indeed, to such an extent has this gone that it drew from Winston Churchill one of his best epigrams when referring to the famous statue of Laocoon and his family destroyed by the serpent he said, 'England is a Laocoon strangled by the old school tie.'

Those Greeks who obeyed the adage 'Nothing too much' had good manners. They were neither flamboyant nor pedestrian. They believed in balance, in a middle course.

This 'old school tie' has spread all over the British Empire. It has very nearly succeeded in turning officials into robots. It has completely succeeded in making ideas in the universities 'bad form.' One is tempted to think that at root the English must have been a nation of the most ostentatious boasters and that it required this discipline of understatement and reticence to make them sociable. When they accuse Americans of being loud-mouthed braggarts they must not forget that originally many Americans came from England, from the England that required all the discipline of the old school tie to shut it up.

Now had it been an admonishment such as the Greeks accepted, 'Nothing too much,' instead of 'nothing at all,' there would have been no need of this suppression.

Nothing too much was the Greeks' equivalent of manners maketh man.

When I visited Greece, I stood on the Acropolis with the late Head Master of Eton College. He was thoughtful as he looked down on the city from which all our culture comes. After gazing long at Athens, he turned to me and asked,

'Would you have sent a son of yours to ancient Athens?' At the risk of being ostracized for ever from his opinion, I answered,

'Certainly not.'

To my relief he replied,

'Neither would I.'

Then he went on to speak of the Athenians of old:

'They had curiosity and flexibility of intellect and an unprecedented sense of beauty. Sparta had discipline only. The Athenians and the Spartans never combined. Had they done so, it would not have been enough. We needed Christianity to make us good neighbors.' From those remarks I realized what the great educator considered necessary to put a man on an equal footing with his fellow men, good neighborliness even to the extent of loving-kindness where called for.

Manners vary with the latitude of a place. There is an island in Polynesia where to be happy is taboo. I know an island where the natives are always merry and bright. The happy mean lies somewhere between these extremes. I think that it will be found where men are considerate and good neighbors.

The Wonder in the Word

When we read a book, how many of us pause to give thanks to these little elves of fantastic shape who deliver lightning to us without delay or misdirection? How many of us are even aware of the little symbols that transmit thought? And yet these are the little messengers that bind the human race together, little heralds that leap over sepulchres and centuries to bring to us ancestral counsel from the mighty men of old. Some of these little characters are as old as leprechauns, as old as the legendary Cadmus who gave them to the Greeks. Those who come from Egypt are still older, as old as their relatives from China which are more numerous and still unchanged. Nearly all our symbols began as pictures, then they became conventional signs, and then people began to make, as it were, puns about those signs – as when the picture of a man with a saw became the past tense of the verb to see. We cannot now detect in our letter B the form of a house, or in our M an owl's ears, because, as the need for these signs increased, they turned into symbols for sounds rather than pictures. We do not realize this because the thought shines through them and shoots silently into our brains; but when someone reads to us, we know that he is turning his symbols into sounds as if they were notes of music. If we knew how to read Chinese, we would find examples of the first beginnings of words when they were still pictures and full of sentiment and poetry. For instance, the word for *peace* is composed by placing the sign for *woman* under the sign for *roof*; and the sign for *happiness*, or rather happiness itself, is suggested by combining the signs for a *son* and *daughter*, implying that a man is happy who possesses a son and a daughter. That is why it is so hard to translate Chinese accurately – for it is as wide as poetry and as hard to confine to one definite and unequivocal meaning. Most of this is concealed in our letters which have become sounds like the wonderful word with which this essay opens, the word *when*. *When* brings to me the sound in passing of the garments of the invisible and taciturn master of our lives, Time. Again it brings

87

to me the image of a hand at the lips, a blown 'Farewell.' It is better in the English language than any language with which I am acquainted, for it has the sound of a whisper in it. If we accept the theory of evolution, which I do not, mankind was advanced when the word *when* was invented through the necessity of recording history and of referring to dates. This brings us to one theory of the birth of words which is that they were the result of an emotional need. Shelley believed in the reverse of this when he wrote:

He gave Man speech and speech created thought
Which is the measure of the Universe.

This is, as you might expect, a theory becoming a poet whether that poet be Plato or Shelley. It is a theory worthy of the dignity of words. It makes words the measure of the universe. This was carried to an extreme by the Nominalists, those subtle thinkers of that earnest phase of human existence, the Middle Ages. There was a time, earlier still, in the fourth century of Christianity, when men engaged in the most subtle exercises of the intellect, in questions, theorems and hair-splitting tenets – an opinionated time when argument tended to become fierce and illiberal in contrast to that more tolerant time at the beginning of the fourth century before Christ when Socrates disputed. Had Socrates lived when the Church Fathers disputed, he might have been exalted with Athanasius or condemned with Arrius, or, as he probably could, have won both orthodox and heresiarch to a third belief more subtle than either *homoousia* or *homoiousia*. But what a gallus time it was when you could be damned for a diphthong, when life hung on a vowel, and the fate of the soul on an iota, literally! Was there ever more wonder in a word?

They who held that nothing existed without a name or a word for it were opposed by the Realists who held the reverse opinion. It was a time when ideas had a vogue: a time when men went to prison for a thought. Men played with words as if they were algebraical signs. This the Irish schoolmen did in the century that gave birth to that pinnacle in a desert of ignorance, Dun Scotus Eirugena. And what they did may be gleaned in the writings of that direct descendant of the Schoolmen, James Joyce. It was a time, later, when Abelard narrowly escaped excommunication; and, later still, when that sanguine youth with the lovely name, Pico della Mirandola, undertook to defend a thousand propositions. It was a period where thought became ingrown, as it were: words, words, words – a period caricatured by Rabelais with his shower of frozen words. In the hands of the Schoolmen, words became celibate and sterile. They were using words for their own sake. They were as fatuous as the ignorant and superstitious people who considered the poet Virgil to be a magician (as indeed he was, but in another sense than theirs) and wore bits of his manuscript as an amulet around their necks. Yes, magician he truly was when he put words together in such a way that they more than became pictures again as in the line in which he describes the Tiber sliding by the antique walls of Rome, a line in which towers are reflected, a line through which the river glides.

'Wielder of the stateliest measure ever moulded by the lips of man.' Some words when put together in a fine frenzy can say more than the sum of them added up. *Airy* and *nothing* are empty enough for all intents and purposes; but when they are employed to describe the function of the magician, meaning the poet, who can:

> Give to airy nothing a local habitation and a name,

we get an idea of how words may be used as a charm. Granted there is more than the effect of mere words at work here; there is the order in which they are placed and the rhythm of that order; but when used with curious happiness, they can bring us messages from

> The prophetic soul of the wide world dreaming of things to come.

They can be themselves prophecies.

II

There is a less exalted and magical level in which words may be used as incantations or charms, which depend for their efficacy chiefly on their sound. I am inclined to the belief that many a savage tribe was helped in its conversion more by the majestic sound of the genitive plurals of the Latin than by an understanding of dogma: *In secula seculorum*. That which is strange and far has a romance all its own, and often because unknown is, strangely enough, an antidote to ignorance. Take the case of scientific medical terms: big words, and complicated, can do far more when it comes to a cure than simple ones. This is due to the fact that fully 50 per cent of every case of illness is psychiatrical. For instance, if you have been kept awake all night with a hacking cough, a pain under the breast bone and a tickling sensation in the throat, and you go to a doctor, does he repeat your symptoms as I have put them? Certainly not! He observes the long descended technique and ritual of the Faculty, and with due solemnity pronounces the word *bronchitis*. You are half cured already! You are immediately made aware of the fact that Jones had it and survived; and that Mrs Klapperhammer was a new woman after the doctors had warned her to conserve her breath. The symptoms have been gathered up and trapped in a word, and divested of much of their dread. You would have felt that you were but scurvily dealt with had the doctor dismissed your case with a simple word in English, just as that irate patient in the insane asylum who was always complaining felt when the doctor said, 'It's only wind.' '*Only* wind?' he roared. 'Have you ever heard of the Tay bridge disaster?'

If you look at the menu in a smart restaurant you will find that the names of the dishes are in French. They immediately assume a quality of refinement, and no matter how heartily you partake of them, thanks to the French you are a gourmet rather than a glutton. A peach tastes sweeter when called by Melba's name. When I think of this, it seems all the more strange to me to recall that the Greeks, who were a sensitive people, used the dialect of the Spartans, which was Doric, on their bills of fare. It is much the same as if we were to use braid Scots and call a pudding with 'concealments' a *haggis* and speak of cabbage as *kail*. I do not know how the Romans enchanted their food, but I am pretty sure that they used the language of Athens, which was to them Parisian Greek.

There is a considerable devotion to bottles in this country. I do not mean those in the drug stores which are semi-concealed and mixed with every commodity save, perhaps, a drug. I am alluding to buildings devoted to the bottle. If you obey the instruction *Pull* on a door and enter the place, you will see on one side of the room a long altar-like structure made of marble or mahogany, and behind it a mirror and ascending shelves. Below there are brightly illuminated cases; these, as well as the shelves, all contain bottles. Bottles rise up on each side of the cash register, shine reflected in the mirror, and send heliographic messages up to you from the cases where they are displayed. Each bottle is gay with a label like a surtout and looks like a knight on horseback when the pourer gives the ensemble the appearance of a horse. Now the particular thing is that, no matter what they hold, no bottle mentions it on label or coat of arms. They call the lovely things of the world to witness, roses and stars and swallows and feathers, and the names of beautiful places and famous men; but of their contents, not a word. Why is this? Why, of course, the word or name is half the effect. It is not generally known that distillers are so well aware of this that there are hundreds and hundreds of names patented on their lists so that no rival can get hold of them and charm their customers away. All the glens of Scotland and bonnie Dundee are on the list. But they never say anything simple or direct. In this way there is growing up a periphrastic literature about drink which I find very charming and encouraging because, when I am drinking, it is to me a proof that those who brew are also tasting the Pierian spring.

> Old Anacreon
>   Was the wine's best poet;
> Had he Inisowen,
>   How his verse would show it!

Inisowen, of course, is Irish whiskey.

III

From words as the names of different kinds of spirits I will turn to words as presentations of the characters of men. You have only to read a line of Milton to realize that you are in the presence of a dignified and lofty spirit, a soul

> That with no middle flight intends to soar
> Above the Aonian mount.

And he was well able to soar in no middle flight, for he was fourth among the world's epic poets. How do his words make you aware of the character of the man? By revealing his style, which was lofty, solemn, and sonorous, and there is nothing trivial or sententious to mar a Biblical solemnity. Indeed, so solemn and religious is it that on one occasion it was used as a prayer by one who had been wrapped all his life in poetry, that cousin of religion. It is told of the poet Yeats that when threatened by shipwreck the captain asked him to recite a prayer; he intoned:

> Of Man's first disobedience and the fruit
> Of that forbidden tree whose mortal taste
> Brought sin into the world and all our woe,
> Sing, heavenly Muse.

The ship was saved.

Words can reveal the man. *Le style est l'homme*. Nevertheless, the style is not every man, for few men possess enough command over words to reveal themselves. Milton can sigh for his own hard lot: his Samson Agonistes, when he makes him lament his hard and hopeless plight in the memorable line, so full of spondees with each set of two syllables eloquent with the resignation of despair:

'Eyeless in Gaza, at the mill, with slaves.'

But the majority of the human race never rises beyond the use of clichés, slang, or some basic form of hackneyed and attenuated phrases. This brings me to another consideration, and that is the abuse of words. Through abuse, words are losing their force. Dean Swift could say 'He is a *mean* man,' and we get the impression of a poor, cowardly, and parsimonious character, a fellow no one would care to meet. Simple English is no longer emphatic enough to please a public that has been pampered by exaggeration. And yet the greatest prose in the English language is simple and trustworthy. Here is an example of it, and of words at their best. It is from North's translation of Plutarch's *Lives of Famous Greeks and Romans*. That perfect knight, the late George Wyndham, called my attention to the passage that describes with merciless and telling simplicity Cleopatra straining to draw Antony up into the monument:

> Notwithstanding, Cleopatra would not open the gates but came to the high windows and cast out certain chains, and ropes, in the which Antony was trussed: and Cleopatra her oune self with two women only which she had suffered to come with her into these monuments, trised Antony up. They that were present to behold it said they never saw so pitiful a sight. For they plucked poor Antony all bloody that he was, and drawing on with the pangs of death, who holding

up his hands to Cleopatra, raised up himself as well as he could. It was a hard thing for these women to do, to lift him up: but Cleopatra stooping down with her head, putting to all her strength to her uttermost power, did lift him up with much adoe and never let go her hold, with the help of the women beneath that bad her be of good corage, and were as sorie to see her labour so as she herself. So, when she had gotten him in after that sort, and laid him on a bed: she rent her garments upon him, slapping her breast and scratching her face and stomake. Then she dried up his blood that berayed his face, and called him her Lord, her husband and Emperor forgetting her miserie and calamity, for the pity and compassion she took of him.

This is dynamic enough but it continues after the countryman came with his basket that carried the asp concealed:

Her death was very sodaine. For those whom Caesar sent unto her ran thither in all haste possible and found the soldiers standing, at the gate, mistrusting nothing nor understanding of her death. But when they opened the doors they found Cleopatra stark dead, layed upon a bed of gold, attired and araied in her royal robes, and one of her two women which was called Iras, dead at her feet; and her other woman called Charmion half dead and trembling, trimming the Diademe which Cleopatra wore upon her head. One of the souldiers seeing her, angrily said to her, 'Is that well done, Charmion?' 'Verie well,' said she again. 'And meet for a Princess discended from the race of so many noble kings.' She said no more, but fell down dead hard by the bed.

Shakespeare takes this word for word and puts it into his incomparable verse, but the prose is well worthy of the verse and the incident is just as dramatic in its own way when related by North as it is on the stage. We see the Queen deprived of majesty straining like a common serving woman with her own hands which never let go their hold, so intense is her will; and then, forgetful of her own 'miserie and calamity' in the paroxysm of her grief; and again within the compass of a few lines she is enthroned, and we are in the royal presence, majestic with her own majesty and that of death.

George Wyndham justly remarked; 'Of good English prose

there is much; but of the world's greatest books in great English prose, there are not many.'

IV

The wonder of words is seen in names. And names seem to denote character.

'We two' she said, 'will seek the groves
   Where Lady Mary is
With her five handmaidens whose names
   Are five sweet symphonies:
Cecily, Gertrude, Margaret, Magdalen and Rosalys.'

Eleanor is a stately name; and what a golden name is that of the young bride in Rome, Aurunculeia, whom Catullus sung. And then there is Beatrice, 'The most exalted lady loved by a man.'

If we turn to that rhymed list of the knights who fought at Agincourt, we come across the greatest names of England, names of the Norman families, some of whom exist today:

Warwick in blood did wade,
Oxford the foes invade
And cruel slaughter made
   Still as they ran up;
Suffolk his axe did ply;
Beaumont and Willoughby
Bare them right doughtily:
   Ferrers and Fanhope.

I can see the plumes in the helmets of Beaumont and Willoughby as they swayed from side to side, dealing death from their horses.

Proper names are often associated with places, as Thomas a Becket or William a Trent, old English names as old as Robin Hood. He was Fitzoud and the 'fitz' which is 'filz,' the natural son of a king, was dropped when he went into the greenwood to join the men the cruel laws of the Normans outlawed. Then there are names with epithets such as Brian of the Tributes, or Conn of the Hundred Battles. The Hundred Fighter, as he is also called, was of course Irish. It is to Ireland one must go to get names so old that any other meaning, if they had another, is lost in the night of time. What does McCarthy mean? Nothing but the men of the clan of Cormac McCarthy, called Great. *Cormac McCarthy Fortis me fieri fecit* is engraved on the great bell in Blarney castle – 'Cormac McCarthy the Great caused me to be made.' It will be noticed that the bell speaks for itself, not, as the frivolous might say, 'obviously because it has a tongue,' but because to bells an individuality is attributed:

> The great bells of the belfry
>   From their prison in the tower,
> Guthlac and Bartholamaeus
>   Proclaimed the midnight hour.

Some of the oldest names in the world have been found on standing stones: 'Fergus, son of Roy, is here.' But for the charm of modern names or, rather, of names used charmingly we must turn to Milton or to Walter Scott. The soft, sliding words that name rivers such as Sweet Afton or Windrush or Evenlode have a charm that comes down from some gentle, prehistoric race, for the names of rivers are the oldest names in a country. It was no set of savages that named the Thames or the Boyne or the lordly Shannon:

> There was the Liffey rolling down the lea,
>   The shadowy Duff, the fishy fruitful Bann,
> The Lordly Shannon, spreading like a sea,
>   Swift Awni Dhu that of the Englishman
> Is called Blackwater . . .

'I wouldn't put it past the Englishman,' as the Gaelic colloquialism goes, to change a lovely name for a pedestrian and matter-of-fact epithet. There are lovely and ugly words: *pavilion* is a lovely word, but *creek* is hateful. If you examine the words that charm, you will find that they have short vowels corresponding to head notes, for instance: 'Hail to thee, blithe spirit.'

Those words make the lark ascend. This is what I mean by the charm of words. What are we to think of the latter day usage of initial letters for names? True, it is born out of convenience; but I hate to think of the trouble and the confusion that awaits archeologists who shall be disinterring us one thousand years hence. What will they make of G.O.P. or W.P.A. or of O.W.I. or of A.W.O.L.? This is an interesting development. It is a new use of letters. They are pictures no longer or even sounds, but the first letters of words that are no longer necessary and may be discarded and forgotten. What a far call is this from the ancient pictures of two women under a roof, and the signs for a son and daughter that connote peace and contentment – without which no one can appreciate the charm of anything.

Poets and Little Children

If you cast your mind back through centuries of English literature you will think it remarkable how little consideration the poets have given to little children. And yet our Christian gospel opens with that tenderest of admonitions, 'suffer little children to come unto me.' The reason the poets were not interested in little children is not that they were all irreligious but that poetry dealt and still deals with the more active times of life when deeds are done and desires move men and women. There is very little poetry about old age; and this fact would seem to bear me out when I say that poetry is for the most part the expression of the dramatic period of life.

Yet there is one remarkable instance of a poet who lived when every day was a moving drama and who had nevertheless the tenderness – for all that he knew of soldiers and adventurers – to suffer little children to come to him. This was the Reverend Robert Herrick, Vicar of Dean Prior deep in rural Devonshire in the south west of England. He was a friend of Ben Jonson and undoubtedly he could not have been such a close friend as he was without being known to Shakespeare, Ben Jonson's comrade. The Reverend Mr Herrick detested 'dull Devonshire' to which he was appointed and from which he but seldom got away. And yet he acknowledged that it was good for his poetry to be left to himself. That he did not neglect his duties as vicar is well known.

When I went to visit his little church in Dean Prior the verger told me that the Reverend Vicar was accustomed to throw his prayer book from the pulpit at a sleeping parishioner. But there was a tender side to him. I like to think of him visiting the cottages and shaking hands with the little children. Had he not felt many a little hand he could not have written how the hands of children are cold as frogs or *paddocks* as they were called in that older English of his day. This is a poem about a baby saying grace before a meal composed by the quick-tempered and kind shepherd of the little flock about Dean Prior:

Here a little child I stand
Heaving up my either hand,
Cold as paddocks though they be,
Yet I lift them up to Thee
For a benison to fall
On our meat, and on us all.

I know no more moving example of pure innocence than that little flower of the imagination, *A Baby's Grace* by Robert Herrick, in all literature. It is so simple and happy. 'Heaving up': the barely co-ordinated motion of a baby's hands!

For the most part poems by other poets about children are far from being happy. Some are so full of anguish as to be insufferable; poems by brokenhearted parents, epitaphs on little children or the tears of a little child who fell asleep after being corrected too sternly by his father. That one was by Coventry Patmore, a poet forgotten at the moment but who is bound in the long run to win the recognition the soundness of both his verse and his principles deserves. Though it is not directly connected with my theme, it is interesting to examine the causes of such a poet's temporary eclipse. George Moore used to say that he deserved oblivion because he made his own wife the heroine of *The Angel in the House*, whereas 'had it been someone else's wife such as Helen of Troy or Iseult or Francesca, he would have been in the great tradition of adultery which is the subject of the greatest poetry in the world.' But George Moore never had an angel in his house so he could not speak from experience. Now to return. I will not quote Robert Bridges', the late Poet Laureate's, poem to his still-born child beginning, 'Perfect little body without fault or strain.' It is too poignant. There is no purgation of anguish in that grief.

There is, in a translation from the Chinese by Arthur Waley, a poem with the title, *Remembering Golden Bells*. A bereaved father is recalling the little childish ways of his baby girl who was taken away from him by death just as he was beginning to understand her baby prattle. He is trying to force his mind back to the time before he was married, to the time before his little Golden Bells was born. The only comfort a bereaved parent can get from this is that his grief is not unique, that it has visited other parents in other lands. It is the consolation common to us all, poor as it is, that we are all in the same boat, on the stream of time, fathers and mothers and Golden Bells.

There is a poem by another bereaved father, Thomas Edward Brown (1830–1897), a dramatic picture so majestic in its sadness and simplicity that it becomes all Aeschylean.

> She knelt upon her brother's grave,
>   My little girl of six years old –
> He used to be so good and brave,
>   The sweetest lamb of all our fold:
> He used to shout, he used to sing,
>   Of all our tribe the little king –
> And so unto the turf her ear she laid,
>   To hark if still in that dark place he played.
>
>> No sound! no sound!
>> Death's silence was profound;
>> And horror crept
>> Into her aching heart, and Dora wept.
>> If this is as it ought to be,
>> My God, I leave it unto Thee.

In these two last lines the whole problem of evil in the world is propounded.

Christina Georgina Rossetti has some lines, 'Is it well with the child?' which are only mentioned because they go to show how mysterious and effective is the above-quoted poem as compared to hers.

Wordsworth's poem about a dead child or little maid is magnificent in another and far from Christian way. The worth of words, as becomes a poet named by the happy chance that resides in the naming of men in English, is exemplified in the sheerness of the lines as the littleness of man in comparison with the awful working of the inanimate machine of nature is set forth:

> No motion has she now, no force,
> She neither hears nor sees,
> Rolled round in Earth's diurnal course
> With rocks and stones and trees.

There is a charming poem by Thomas Ashe entitled *Meet No Angels, Pansie*. It is about a little girl:

> She said, 'We meet no angels now,'
> And soft lights streamed upon her;
> And with white hand she touched a bough;

She did it that great honor: –
What! meet no angels, Pansie?

How could she have known that she was one herself? It is a sweet poem and full of light and gaiety; but the maid is almost grown up. She is not in the little children's class as is this child in a poem by my friend Dermot Freyer. It is fit to be read side by side with the first poem I have quoted about the baby whose hands were 'cold as paddocks.' The baby's hands in this poem may have been cold but they were also dimpled:

Little Dolly Dimplekin
Has dimples on her cheek and chin;
And dimples on her knuckles, too:
Which show that Dolly's years are few.

Here is a piece which sets a little girl running in a meadow golden with buttercups. She is made into the spirit and personification of the golden things in Nature, the gold of the meadows, the gold of the fruit, the gold of the leaf. And to give these things life she is made to run in the sunshine. And she is isolated by the simple device on the part of the poet of closing the eyes and seeing in the mind's eye only her. Thus is the stillness produced which the powder of the buttercups can dust with gold.

Golden stockings you had on
In the meadow where you ran;
And your little knees together
Bobbed like pippins in the weather,

When the breezes rush and fight
For those dimples of delight,
And they dance from the pursuit,
And the leaf looks like the fruit.

I have many a sight in mind
That would last if I were blind
Many verses I could write
That would bring me many a sight.

Now I only see but one,
See you running in the sun,
And the gold dust coming up
From the trampled buttercup.

It may seem strange that the myriad-minded Shakespeare found little room or evinced little interest in little children. I confess that it did seem passing strange to me that he whose understanding of humanity was so mighty interpreted the ways and aspirations of little children hardly at all. Did his infinite tenderness fail? I searched and searched and finding little to quote I ran round a few blocks to ask my friend Granville Barker who has interpreted and studied the poet more than most actors and producers. He will tell me why it is that a hiatus Herrick filled so well was never seemingly apparent to the supreme poet. It is pleasant to think that New York is getting the attributes of a city at last, that it is a place where the people who are interested in culture and civilization may be found grouped within easy reach of each other. Granville Barker is round the corner so to speak. So, too, is Charlie Towne and not a block away, John Erskine. I asked the great Shakespearian why Shakespeare had written so little about children. He turned the question with a smile. 'He had too much trouble trying to make them into actors to have anything left to say about them.' It must not be forgotten that children in Elizabethan days acted the parts of women.

The poet Burns' brave lines to his illegitimate daughter are tender and defiant. He wishes her all her mother's graces and none of her poor daddy's faults. And it is through a recognition of the place of children in the scheme of life that he rises beyond the pedestrian poetry of everyday and gives us his philosophy –

> To make a happy fireside
> For weans and wife
> Of human life
> Is the true pathos and sublime.

Yeats comes to the same conclusion as he ponders upon the meaning of existence and gives us his opinion on it. We expect poets to give us their opinion on life and on what it is all about. We await them with interest because from poets we are more likely to get original views than from preachers. Yeats sings:

> For all Life has to give us is
> A child's laughter, a woman's kiss.

He comes to the same conclusion as Burns.

Since this is so when we review all that poets have written

101

about children we are inclined to wonder why they devoted more time and rhyme to their deaths than to their mirthful days. I suppose it is because the greatest tragedy on earth is the death of a child: the gold head dust; the blossom blighted. That even the most fierce and savage heart can feel. There is an example of the rough heart of the slayer softening when he saw his handiwork, in the ballad *Edom o'Gordon*. In the absence of her Lord, the Castle of the Rodes is besieged by Edom o Gordon and the ground wall stone pulled out and the castle filled with smoke. The little child cries out not knowing what it all means. In order to save her from suffocation her mother rolls her in sheets and throws her over or 'owre' the wall. The castle is on fire:

> They rowed her in a pair o'sheets
>   And tow'd her owre the wa'
> But on the point o'Gordon's spear
>   She gat a deadly fa'.
>
> O bonnie, bonnie was her mouth
>   And cherry were her cheiks
> And clear, clear was her yellow hair
>   Whereon the red bluid drieps.
>
> Then with his spear he turned her owre;
>   O gin her face was wane!
> He said 'Ye are the first tha' e'er
>   I wished alive again.'
>
> He turned her owre and owre again;
>   O gin her skin was white!
> 'I might hae spared that bonnie face
>   To haie been some man's delight.'

This is one of the greatest dramatic ballads ever written. You hear the savage becoming remorseful through his own admission and through that you see the beauty that was slain. That turning 'owre and owre' again with his spearpoint as he examined her! And the savage admission, 'Ye are the first tha' e'er I wished alive again.' It is terrific.

The question why poets have dwelt on the deaths of children goes deeper than I know. Perhaps it is because great poetry becomes in a way religious. And religion dwells more on death than on that other cosmic thing which is germane to it, love.

102

However it be, they have but one consolation to offer which in fact amounts to a distrust or a disbelief in life. They tell us that the dead little ones are like the youth whom the water nymph drew down to her home below the pool, saved 'From the slow poison of pitiless Time.' Poor; but what other consolation can laymen give? Nevertheless, past the epitaphs, I love to go back to that sturdy little fellow who 'heaved' up his little cold fists and prayed for a blessing on us all.

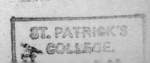

How the Poets Praised Women

The best poets are they who praised women best. It is my belief that literature, and certainly poetry which is the first form of literature, waxes and wanes with the position woman holds. The higher her position, the greater the regard and respect in which she is held, the better the literature.

How is it, I wonder, that the modern poets praise women no more? Is it the fault of the poets – or of the women? Both. Since women, through Mrs Pankhurst, Suffragettes and Company, claimed and gained 'equality,' woman's position in poetry has been steadily on the wane. They are our equals now and would, I am afraid, regard it as a slight if we attempted to return them to their pedestal. There was a time, and it is a time I like to linger in, when they were our superiors. So then were we, the writers, superior – we who find our delight in beauty, and both beauty and inspiration in women? As Goethe says, 'the eternal feminine leads us on . . .' which, from a poet's point of view, is the ideal situation in which to find himself.

And while on this subject of praise, let me say that I hold it a duty to praise the beautiful. Loveliness is on the wing, and this club-car in which we find ourselves is running fast to a silent destination. Therefore, not a moment should be lost in giving praise to the beautiful (praise helps to increase their beauty), even though the beauty seems untranslatable. For even the immortal Yeats lamented the fact that no poet could ever describe the beauty of a woman or stars in words that would hold against their actual appearance. Therefore, he bowed down his heart and sang of his adoration, rather than of his lady.

But for all that, it is through poetry that one really detects the quintessence of a woman. Out of the silent ages, a face, a point of view, a mannerism will come through and bring some Mistress Isabelle sharply into focus . . . the creaking sandals of the majestic lady Catullus loved, the white arms of Nausicaa, the whole measure of Villon's pretty little friend, whose entire conversational repertoire consisted of 'Is that so . . .'

In the grand and classic manner, Homer praised his ladies less by describing their features (for these he had stock adjectives) than by giving you an intuition of a world of which they were a part – and which they made comely, sweet and wholesome. Occasionally, as in the case of the delicious Calypso, she 'of the braided tresses,' he goes beyond the stock adjective 'fair' to create a picture for the inner eye . . . 'clad her in a shining robe, light of woof and gracious, and about her waist she cast a fair girdle, and a veil withal upon her head.' Homer was not a woman's poet. Horace's praise was the sophisticated appreciation of a philanderer for an entertainer, or a dancing-girl. I dare not draw the conclusion . . .

The question of why women like to be praised at all by poets was put to me the other day. (Certainly, it was not one I would put to myself!) I can only suggest that they like to be praised by a poet because he can lift them beyond the narrow precincts of their personality and give their individuality a significance in Eternity . . . endow their features, qualities, idiosyncracies, with a cosmic interpretation. It may be that poets have an eye for the overlooked beauty – the unstandardized – and an unconscious intuition of what is worth recording in time.

Villon, for instance, gave a kind of florid, aromatic beauty to Bertha Big Foot. Sappho immortalizes the realistic, exasperating slovenliness of her little friend who was forever dragging her robe untidily about her ankles. Chaucer, too, that sweet well of 'English undefiled,' dared to praise in unaccepted regions. Chaucer, who kept his pretty praise for private application. We hear of his being blamed, as Dante was, for the laxity of his morals. These he projected (as ego-protection, if you will) onto the Wife of Bath, one of the most real and bewitching women of the world, when the world was merry and rollicking withal. One might say he expressed his views from behind her petticoats.

I should imagine that any woman's choice of a poet by whom to be praised would be Shakespeare. (If she could be quite sure it would be praise she would receive.) His was the greatest and most versatile capacity for praise, and venom. Who else could sing as sweetly, 'Mistress mine, where are you roaming?' . . . and conceive the unsurpassable phrase, 'sweet and twenty?' Who, too, could voice bitterness such as his towards that mysterious dark lady with her proclivity for infidelity?

Aye, and by Heaven one would do the deed,
Though Argus were her eunuch and her guard.

Surely the women of Shakespeare's day must have been
superb. Not the gentle 'Angel in the House' of the Victorian
era, nor yet like Beatrice, 'the most exalted lady loved by man,'
but full of the very versatility Shakespeare mirrored. So, too,
must their position have been high to win from the poet Brown
such noble and honest appreciation as the Dowager Countess
of Pembroke did:

Sidney's sister, Pembroke's mother;
Death, when thou hast slain another
Fair and learn'd and wise as she
Time shall throw a dart at thee.

Here was something added, something subtracted, from the
exalted passion of Dante who swooned for love of Beatrice
when he was nine, and cried out that 'the city sat solitary' for
him when she was away from Florence. Dante was the turning
point in European culture, a majestic troubadour from those
delicious Courts of Love, where minstrels, jongleurs and
troubadours held forth, and each lady had 'one or two lovers
besides her own dear lord.'

Dante represented the transition from flesh to spirit. He was
the first great poet to lift his head, and the loveliness of women,
above the ages, since the advent of Christianity. Through
Beatrice he expressed the new ideal. It is Beatrice who led him
up through the Seventh Heaven to the core of the inverted
Mystic Rose . . . who endowed him with the power to ascend
Paradise. Scoffed at by his contemporaries, Guido in particular, for the disparity between his way of living and the ideals he
expressed, he found salvation in his worship, through Beatrice,
of the Blessed Virgin. As Yeats wrote:

He found the unpersuadable justice and he found
The most exalted lady loved by man.

One is loath to speak knowingly of Dante, for mine is one of
the little *barques* he warns off from his 'singing keel' when he is
about to begin that voyage to Paradise. How is it, that, though
he wrote the greatest love poem in the world and of 'the most
exalted lady loved by man,' Dante, like Homer, is not a
woman's poet?

'Like a bubble sung out of a linnet's lung' are the lyrics of Burns, masterpieces of spontaneity and simplicity whose praise is indirect, but unlike Homer, intimate and full of wonder.

Oh saw ye bonnie Leslie
As she gaed o'er the border?
She's gone like Alexander
To spread her conquests further.

This is an immeasurably greater tribute to bonnie Leslie than Petrarch's to his Laura who 'evaporates in praise.' Surely no lady would give thanks for that!

Now it would ill become me if I omitted my own countrymen from a catalogue of such praise. If excuse were needed I might fall back on the old metrical maxim:

For acuteness and valour the Greeks,
For excessive pride the Romans,
For dullness the creeping Saxons,
For beauty and amourousness the Gaels.

Yeats writes, in praise of women, that he is unable to praise them. The women, shaped and given flesh by his imagination, are too transcendental; they are women of moonlight and dreams. Of such a one he writes:

Oh cloud-pale eyelids, dream-dimmed eyes,
The poets labouring all their days
To build a perfect beauty in rhyme
Are overthrown by a woman's gaze.

More than a thousand years ago, some unknown chronicler labored, too, to build a perfect beauty in rhyme in honor of Etain, the Fair.

Now the High King of Ireland was going over the green of Bri Leith, and he saw, at the side of a well, a woman with a bright comb of gold and silver, and she was washing in a silver basin, having four golden birds on it, and little bright purple stones set in the rim . . . she had on her a dress of green silk . . . and the sunlight falling on her hair was like the yellow flags in summer, or like the red gold after it has been rubbed. Her soft hands were as white as the snow of a single night, her eyes as blue as any blue flower, and her lips as red as the berries of the rowan tree, and her body as white as the foam of a wave. The bright light of the moon was in her face, and the highness of pride in her eyebrows, the light of wooing in her eyes, and when she walked she had the step that was steady and even like the walk of a queen.

What brightness has left the earth! And what relish of glad color and the pride of life!

It is hard to praise, or even describe, the modern woman. In her dream of herself, she is making, even as we look, a new kind of beauty. It may take years before the type which woman is creating for herself becomes hereditary, legendary, and evident to the poets, who are still dreaming of the 'face that launched a thousand ships.' As I have not many acquaintances, I have to be satisfied with the visions of this new loveliness which is materialized in the mannequins in the windows of great stores. I know a most modern beauty in a central avenue.

She has a most disdainful air,
And hollow cheeks and long-lashed eyes,
And shoulders flat and high and square;
Her poise is cold and wordly wise.
One hand pulls on the other's glove
With arms of aluminum;
Her loins could make a townsman love;
But could not make a Dutchman's home.

It is a difficult and austere beauty, languid, distinguished and artificial. And I, for one, do not object to the artifice, for the poet said, 'One must labor to be beautiful.' She is a priestess of Beauty . . . even when it is only her own. Meanwhile, all a poet can do is to be ever on the alert for beauty, and be ready to 'praise whatever is well made.'

Culture and Continuance

There is a city of my heart from which we may learn that, although our modern life is bound up with speed and movement, speed and movement cannot replace Thought and are not necessarily synonymous with Progress and Civilization.

I know a town where there is neither coal nor oil. That town is Dublin, the capital of that part of Ireland which is neutral and which, owing to its neutrality, has neither friends nor enemies, nor fuel. Strange, the first thing that strikes me about Dublin is most pleasant and surprising; my ears and eyes seem improved beyond belief. I can hardly believe my eyes, and my ears are supersensitive. I was about to attribute my improved vision to some virtue, or, failing that, to some vitamin in myself, until I found that my keener sight was due to the crystal air. Where there is no coal, the atmosphere cannot be polluted. My acuter hearing was due to the fact that my ears were healing from the barbaric and debasing noises of the Century of Speed.

The loudest sound I heard was that of the trotting of cab horses, if I except the shrill screams of a newsboy, a shrillness that was merely a matter of pitch. How could I distinguish pitch in the twentieth century wherein they batter your ears with megaphones, or those misnamed instruments which are called microphones, though they magnify into outrage every sound?

The candles on the dinner-table tonight need not be waxen. Paraffin candles will burn just as mellowly and accustom the eye to their soothing light. Every woman is improved by candlelight; and, if it were not for their crimson nails, I could imagine by candlelight that I saw alive and graceful the hands that Gainsborough and Romney painted. Of one thing I am certain: to-night I shall listen entranced, not to the deadly audibility of the twentieth century, but to voices as sweet and low as the *gentil babil* which so nearly undid Parsifal.

I have been invited to stay with a friend who lives one hundred miles away. There was a time when I could run down to lunch with him and be back comfortably in half a day. Now I shall have to take the morning mail coach and consider myself lucky, since the weather is fine, if I can get an outside seat. These coaches are high enough to enable the traveller to look over walls and hedges and see what goes on on the lawns of the country mansions. I will stop a night at some village hotel, one of those that have been bypassed since the coming of the automobile, a hostelry at which none of those who was 'going places' has thought of visiting.

There is something very tranquillizing in the hoofbeat of horses. I am sitting beside the driver on the box seat. He is purring to his steeds, which he calls by name very softly; and the admiration in the eyes of the greatest horse copers in the world as we pass is a thing to set one at peace with oneself. How much better it is than the scowl of malice that meets the automobile driver, shot at him by men who walk the roads. I notice with admiration the driver's coat with its three capes to keep off rain and snow. They can not sell shoddy to a coachman. It is his uniform; and the mills where it was spun spin stuff to wear long and not out.

Is this the best hotel? It has the largest yard, and we are stopping at it to-night. I wait until everyone has dismounted. Then we walk the horses and coach through the great gate. The hostlers are with us, and they murmur to the horses, calling each by name as they lead them off by the nose. Next morning I awake to a reek of turf smoke which comes from the kitchen. When I go downstairs I see some of the passengers already drinking at the bar. A journey by coach still retains its adventure for eighteenth-century travellers.

Now don't take me for a mystic, because I am one; and, if you judge my problem by that only, you may let whatever prejudice you may have against mystics blind you to a factual problem, which is this: Have you ever noticed that time in some places is different from time in other places? Let me put my cards on the table. I assure you that time in New York is only half as long as time in parts of Europe.

This may be explained by the greater 'extraversions,' to use the new lingo, the greater outward distractions of a great city. But that is not what I mean. I mean that time actually is shorter, and life in time is shorter in New York than in an eighteenth-century country. There is something profound in this to be solved by a philosopher. Meanwhile, without reiterating, I adhere to my thesis: Time is only half as long in New York as elsewhere, and the moon lasts only a fortnight. The fact that New York is on about the forty-second degree of latitude, and Dublin on about the fifty-second, may have something to do with it, but it is happening meanwhile. It is not a subjective thing.

Soon we were on our way and before long had arrived at my host's house. It was one of those to be found all through the eighteenth-century countries: stone-built, ancestral, ornamented, self-contained. Though he had an electric-light installation, the want of fuel sent him back to candles and fires in the evening, instead of central heating. There is a lot to be said for candlelight and firelight; some of the greatest achievements of history have been accomplished in their glow.

What struck me most was mine host's manner. He received me with a grave and affectionate courtesy so far different from the shouting welcomes of our time. I seemed to be meeting the Vicar of Wakefield. He let his man show me to my room. 'We will meet in the library for a little sherry.'

If you do not permit facetiousness to interpose itself, that week seemed as good as a month to me, so firmly rooted had my life become. In myself, too, a deep change was apparent. In the library I took down *The Spectator*, and I found myself wondering if the highest expression of which the English language is capable had not been reached by Steele and Addison. After dinner I found that I could understand and be diverted by a joke from *Punch*. And, contrariwise, I tried to guess what Dr Johnson would have made of *The New Yorker* with which it takes a foot on the accelerator to keep up. *Punch* and *The New Yorker* are exemplars of their respective centuries.

When the eighteenth century, with all its purposefulness, catches up with us, give it a welcome. It has character to offer us which is enduring; and the stability of the home and the inspiration of localitites; and wisdom to transmit that teaches that thought cannot be replaced by movement and speed, and that speed and movement are not always synonymous with progress and civilization.

I Like to Remember

In the days before the invention of writing, the history of the tribe or clan, the exploits of the chieftains, and the pedigrees of the families (on which the title to land depended) all had to be held in the mind of the historian. This historian was invariably a bard. It can hardly be doubted that, in order to help memory, rhythm was invented. And it was Aeschylus who said that memory is the Mother of the Muses – here the Muse of epic and lyric poetry.

In every period of civilization, there have been methods and nostrums for improving the memory. That which helps the memory most is interest in the subject. The next best help is association of ideas. In fact, without association of ideas it is almost impossible to remember. There is little or none of this association in proper names, which are easily forgotten, though the individual be remembered. How often has that imbecile and unapprehended bore, with his grinning 'I know you don't know who I am!' proved this? If any more proof be wanted of the difficulty of dispensing with associated ideas when trying to memorize, let anyone try to repeat this jingle from the unfamiliar language of the Basque two or three days after reading it as many times as he likes, say ten:

Shibbidy, shibbidy,
Tischa ling,
Tomba, tomba,
Bousconchillio,
Coca, mako, tara, ja,
Kreiss, krass, palio,
Shouka, shouka, lina, lina,
Quishon, Kashon,
Toupin.

Presumably, this is some child's catch, like 'Eena, meena, mina, mo.' But how infinitely harder to remember, for we are too old to learn by rote, and it has no rhyme or familiar rhythm. It might as well be a selection of names from some outlandish telephone directory.

Blank verse is a very great aid to memory because it has an underlying sound-rhythm, pattern or channel which leads you to expect something that will fit and flow into it. Music provides another example of how memory can be cultivated. Conductors who go through whole symphonies or concertos are witnesses of what must seem to the uninitiated to be prodigies of memory. In both cases, poetry and music, we have examples of how in turn the Mother of the Muses is aided by her children. Undoubtedly, memory can be aided. It may even be developed in childhood by learning things by rote.

I must confess that I can remember only poems. I can't remember prose. No fault of mine, but the death of my father when I was twelve and a half years old caused me to be sent to a 'boarding-school' – to a series of boarding-schools in Ireland and England, from which I was not to escape for almost seven years.

One of them was conducted by a black-a-vised man who was said to have been crossed in love, and so he entered a community of celibates who took, alas, to teaching boys. This is what he gave us for dictation: 'Sorrow for the dead is the only sorrow from which we refuse to be divorced. Every other wound we seek to heal, every other suffering to forget, this wound alone we cherish and keep open.'

The quotation is not accurate. It could not be. Instead of that interest in a subject which is one of the helps to memory, this filled me at that early age with gloom and revulsion, with intimations of the tomb. It did more: It made me totally incapable of remembering prose of any description. And that is why, though I can remember verses which I love, I should have to select a building in which there would be a prebendary to prompt me if I were asked to recite in public the simplest prayer.

Mercifully I have forgotten my seven years at school.

But I remember poems because there are certain rhythm-hungry cells in, maybe, everyone's mind, else why should song have lasted since the beginning of our history? These cells or patterns or moulds have to be filled. Let me give an example of the opposite to the Basque jingle or catch, an example of a pattern of verse which everyone can remember and retain after one reading:

Christopher Robin goes hoppety, hoppety,
Hoppety, hoppety, hop.
Whenever you ask him politely to stop it, he
Says he can't possibly stop.

This is nonsense verse, but it achieves so completely the task of filling, and of satisfying, the 'fantastic pannicles' of the brain that it is well-nigh unforgettable.

But what about poems that are far from being nonsense verses? Well, here is another confession. When I want to quote a poem, no matter what the length may be, I can only remember it if it is brave, gallant, and – how will I term it? – magnifying. It must do one good to hear it, and do me good to repeat it. Though Poetry cannot be defined any more than a thrill can be defined – it can be only felt – I had the temerity to attempt to define it. It was no more than an attempt, for it was inadequate as a definition; but it was better than 'The right words in the right place,' for this might apply to a gas ration card. It makes no allowance at all for emotion, not even for the emotion that may arise from a filling station. But if it be not a satisfactory definition, my attempt may serve as an illustration of what the kind of poetry must be if I am to remember it. It must be 'a rhythmic spell to enlarge the spirit.'

Enlarge is used in two senses here – in the sense of to *magnify*; and in the sense of to *set free*, as when we say that the stag was 'enlarged,' or when we speak, as Richard Lovelace does, of 'enlarged winds that curl the flood.' And it must be rhythmic, and none of your modern disarticulated prose, which is called *vers libre*. I cannot tell whether it should appeal more to the ear or to the eye. 'To have seen is to know,' as the Greek verb proves; and poetry is largely in its early and simpler form, *optical*; it is invented by the Homeric eye. With this in mind, I once wrote a short article, which I promptly mislaid. It purported to give a few outstanding examples of what is rare in poetry, a line or two that makes the page open and enables you to see with the poet's vision as from a magic casement. Example:

But hark, the cry is 'Astur!'
And, lo, the ranks divide:
And the great Lord of Luna
Comes with his stately stride.

We can see him with his great sword hanging down his back, full six feet long.

Another example is not so full of pride, but it is full of space and feeling. It is from the blind poet Raftery's 'County of Mayo.' Raftery, who composed in Irish at the beginning of the last century, has had the luck to be translated by one of the finest lyric poets of our time, James Stephens. Raftery gets restless at the beginning of the spring. He longs to visit his own county and stop a night on the way, 'And sleep with decent men. And then go on to Balla for a month and drink galore.' But that is not where we see as from a magic casement. It is where his thoughts outrun his feet:

> I say and swear my heart lifts up like the lifting of a tide;
> Rising up like the rising wind till storm and mists must go
> When I remember Carra and Gallen close beside,
> And the Gap of the Two Bushes and the wide plain of Mayo.

He knew where to find it along the highway, and if he could not see the 'wide plain' with its sheep and limestone and grey rain, he could feel the wind from it upon his face through the Gap.

The last example comes from a far more sophisticated poet, yet he had the vision. He had leant from the casement:

> And frosts are slain and flowers begotten,
> And in green underwood and cover
> Blossom by blossom the Spring begins.

The last line is the magic and visionary one. It makes you see the crocuses breaking through the snow.

Then there is a Scots ballad, and ballads are the great quarry whence pure Parian poetry may be hewn. A Scots freebooter is attacking the stronghold of the Gordon, having had an understanding with the wife of the Gordon. The way he is introduced makes you forgive him. He comes with his pipers, playing a march to battle in the dark before the dawn.

> Down Deeside came Inverary whistlin' and playin'.
> He knocked loud at Brackley gate e'er the day dawin'.

He kills Gordon and his brother and remains with the widow. There is a fine example of a magic casement as he is going off the next morning.

> In her chamber she kept him till morning grew gray.

Through the dark woods of Brackley she showed him the
way.
'That fair hill,' said she, 'wi' the sun shinin' on,
Is the Hill o'Glentanner. One kiss and begone!'

You can see the morning sun on the peak: a landmark. He
must have come out by the back way. He found his way easily
enough at the beginning of the ballad.

One of the loveliest images in all the language is from
Spenser's wedding song, made for his wife in lieu of the
wedding presents which were sunk or 'commandeered' on their
way to Youghal in the South of Ireland, a likely place for an
Englishman to lose things.

Like unto Maia whenas Jove her took
In Tempe lying on the flowery grass,
Twixt sleep and wake, after she weary was
With bathing in the Acidalian brook.

Memorizing may be telepathy from the bards of old seeking
a mouthpiece in a sympathizer; but, as for the mechanics of
memory, it cannot be forced. If you force it, it will go like a
pencil through the page, and all is blurred. And it is unconscious; that is to say, you cannot tell how you learned. You may
have read the poem half a dozen times, pointed it out to a
friend, or heard it recited, and, lo, it has got into your mind. If
it has got in inaccurately, the wrong version is very hard to
correct. If you take too much pains to be accurate, the whole
thing may elude you. It is almost impossible to be precise,
seeing that the mood into which you have to throw yourself in
order to memorize or to recite is very like the mood of sleep,
that procreant time in which problems are solved while you are
unconscious.

This has also some bearing on the psychology of memory.
When I want to remember a poem of any length, I get myself
out of the way; that is – I allow my mind to become as blank as
possible, so that there may be nothing to obstruct the flow of
rhyme. This need for inducing a receptive mood may account
for the invocation of the Muse with which the great poets of the
elder day began:

'Sing, Goddess Muse, the direful wrath.'
'Descend from Heaven, Urania.'
'O, buono Apollo!'

116

Only it is in reverse: I do it to remember, not to create.

I said that it is easy to remember brave and cheerful staves. I love to think of the beginning of English poetry when it had a good conscience and England was Merrie England.

'It is a merrie mornyng,' quoth Litel John,
  'By Him who died on tree,
A merrier man than I am one
  Lives not in Christiante.'

'Pluck up thy heart, my dear Master,'
  Litel John can say,
'And think it is a full fair time
  In a mornyng of May.'

Yes, it was a full fair time when not a leaf fell from the greenwood, when:

The wood wele sang and would not cease,
  Sitting upon a spray.

Ah, happy, happy, boughs that cannot shed
  Your leaves, nor ever bid the Spring adieu.

Who dare forget that?

Green Thoughts

To the men who gave the early names to colors -- and there were but few colors to the people of Homer's day -- the word for green was *chloros*, a word we still use in *chlorine* gas and *chlorophyll*, the green of the leaf. The green that was called *chloros* was the early green of the opening buds of oak or beech, the green of the little leaves as they first caught the sunlight. This fresh green of Spring has yellow in it as if the sunlight had melted into the leaf. It is a tender green. If you think of the word tender, you will see how suitable it is when applied to green for deep in it is the picture of young leaves extending their little hands to the warm winds and the light of the new year. To us there is a promise of freshness, growth and resuscitation in green. We feel far more than we can know; and man felt when he saw the first mists of green in field or wood that the wintry death had departed from the earth and that all would be renewed. Dark boughs that were stiff with frost put out green shoots and bend lissomely to the breeze when 'Earth unto its leaflet tips Tingles with the Spring.'

Without green, the green of chlorophyll, there could be no animal life on earth. Even in the treeless places where the Esquimaux live their lives depend on the green algae on which the seals browse.

When you come to think of it, a comparatively small portion of the earth is belted with green. The oceans take up five times more of the earth's surface than the land; and the land is desert in great expanses and so devoid of greenery, or if there be greenery, it is the green of palms. I must confess that I do not like palms for, at the back of my mind, I am afraid of deserts and desiccated places. I could not be an Arab for half a day.

I regret that the Coast, meaning the coast of southern California, is green only for a few weeks in the year and that in some places the green of the mountains is interrupted by clearings to protect the woods from forest fires so that the hills look like herring bones. The green I love is the green of broad-leaved trees, oak, ash, holly, beech, chestnut, maple, elder, apple and even of the strangling ivy. When I was a youth, I could see hundreds of shades of green in 'a vernal wood.' That is because I was born in the greenest spot on earth, in the Green Isle compared to which the green of England as seen from the Channel is a murky yellow. I know that this reveals a hypersensitive disposition and that psychoanalysts aver that there is something wrong with a man who is oversensitive to green.

Green is a promise. It is a promise of abundance and peace. It is not without some mystical significance that the complimentary color of green is red.

Green is the bounteous giver of good things. It is worthier than gold. It requires moisture and warm winds to make a landscape truly green, so green that you could be sure that if a cottage stood in its midst all the children (and there would be many) would have fair skin and rosy cheeks. Trefoil would grow here and cattle stand udder-deep in meadow grass.

Green, green, green is the note of the simplest ballads of England: green woods, green grass and Lincoln green. The ballads of Robin Hood revel in greenery:

In sumer when the shaws be shene
    And leaves be large and long,
Hit is full mery in fair forest
    To hear the briddis song;

To see the deer draw to the dale
    And leave the hilles hee;
And shadow him in the green forest
    Under the greenwood tree.

To me there is nothing lovelier than a drenched wood in May, for I believe that every lovely hue is but the shadow of something supernal and that the heart of this is green, the food of all flowers and of life itself.

An Amazing Coincidence

Castleforbes stands very nearly in the middle of Ireland, in a large park beside Lough Forbes on the River Shannon. Though an old foundation and in the family of Lord Granard for centuries, it is one of the most up-to-date palaces in the country. It is more like a millionaire's palace in Long Island or Newport than an old Irish fortification. The reason for this is that Lady Granard is an American, and she likes to have things up-to-date, especially in her house and in its dairies. If the castle ever had a ghost, modern improvements may have driven him or her out; but it has not become altogether dissociated from the supernatural – I can give it no other term – as this story will show.

One morning my wife and I were about to get into our automobile, and were saying good-by to Lord Granard, who had come out with us to the gravel drive on which the car was standing ready for the resumption of its journey to the far west of Ireland. We had spent the week-end at Castleforbes. Suddenly he said: 'Wait a moment, I have a little present for you.'

He turned and signed to two footmen. After some delay they appeared, straining under the weight of a life-sized figure of an Indian priestess or goddess made of some very heavy wood, for the men could hardly carry the statue.

I looked at the approaching 'present.'

'Is it not enough to enjoy your hospitality over the week-end, without carrying off the furniture?' I asked.

'Wait,' he said. 'There is a pair of them.'

I protested as the men lifted the first onto the back seat of our open car. While they were carrying out the second figure, which was a replica of the first, except that it was turned in a direction opposite to the first, as if the statues were intended to sit in a prayerful attitude on each side of an altar, he said in answer to my reluctance to accept such valuable gifts: 'Her Ladyship does not like them. She considers them to be unlucky.'

Well, I thought, so instead of accepting a gift from him I'm doing him a favor in taking the unlucky statues away. Then it dawned upon me.

'But I don't want them either, if they are unlucky,' I said.

Very unlucky they must be indeed, I said to myself, when an unsuperstitious American woman feels that there is something uncanny about having such things in her house. These must be the substitutes for any ghost that haunted the palace until improvements unhoused him. On my wife's suggestion that it was only Lord Granard's way of conferring a present without making too much of a compliment of it, I got into the car and started away, waving good-by, with the two squatting goddesses or priestesses facing each other on the seat behind us. As I said, they were life-sized. They were seated Indian fashion with their feet gathered up underneath them, their hands joined and raised in prayer and turned, one to the left and one to the right. A red-colored garment covered half their bosoms and went down in a diagonal direction to be caught under their knees. Their skin was the color of ivory, or of some almost-brown egg. On the center of the forehead of each was a caste mark in red. It looked like a clove or a little dagger. They sat comfortably in the back seat on their heavy bases, tilted back a little to prevent their falling forward from a sudden application of the brakes.

On we drove through the brightening morning. Silver mists rose from the park and revealed large emus grazing and tilting up their ostrich heads to survey the strange sight of a modern Mercedes, mahogany and yellow, carrying two antique goddesses of some ancient and unknown or forgotten cult. The great gates opened, and we turned west for Athlone and the Shannon, and for Connemara far beyond. It was about eight o'clock of a summer's morning. The dew was drying rapidly. The day promised to be fine. Barring accidents, we should be at home before noon.

On the good and rather straight road we were dawdling along at a quiet eighty. The statues stood it well. Probably they had never passed through the air at such a rate since they left Mandalay – I had an idea that it was from Mandalay they had been taken. When we came to the bridge over the Shannon, they passed out of my mind, which was occupied with many things at the same time as is usually the case with that mysterious thing, the mind. I was trying to admire the white sheen of the spreading river, and simultaneously to steer clear

121

of the donkey carts and the unpredictable movements of cattle coming into the market town. Then the road surface began to deteriorate. High speed is rather dangerous on an Irish road because of the gates that open out from fields and are concealed by the dense hawthorn hedges that fence these pastures. So I slowed down to about thirty-two miles. Fifteen miles west of Athlone is the town of Ballinasloe on the river Suck. There is a saying that once you are west of the Shannon you may say anything that comes into your head and 'get away with it'; but west of the Suck you may do anything you damned well please. There is a great lunatic asylum at Ballinasloe – one of the largest in the country. It is an enclosed asylum, for of course the whole of Ireland is an open-air lunatic asylum: hence its charm. I should have remembered what was on the back seats when I saw the people staring at us in Ballinasloe; but I put their curiosity down to their environment. On we drove. From a ridge we caught a sudden glimpse of the Twelve Bens of Connemara standing amethystine in the morning light. The mountains of home!

If you turn north at Recess you take about twenty miles off the journey, and you see some magnificent lake, island and mountain scenery as you pass along the Valley of Lough Inagh. After twelve miles of this you resume the western road through the lovely Pass of Kylemore, where a castle bought with the money of another American, Miss Zemmermann, who married the Duke of Manchester, stands reflected in its lake. This lake is prized for its salmon and sea trout. Everyone who pays a license is not entitled to fish in Ireland. In addition, you have to pay to rent a preserved lake. Some of the lakes and rivers in Ireland cost more than five thousand dollars for the fishing season. Kylemore Lake is not so expensive, but it cannot be had for nothing. I held half of it, and so I know.

Along the part of Kylemore Lake which lies to the south runs a straight sandy road. The surface is firm but rolling, so that if you put on speed your car leaps up and down. But the view is unimpeded and you can bowl along. We were bowling along at about fifty, for we knew that there were no side gates at this place. Suddenly out of a hedge where no gate had been came a saloon car driven by a liveried chauffeur. I blew the horn and the man stopped with his wheels locked hard to the right. I could see the tires of his left front wheel standing well out of the mud guard. He was trying to turn right, but when he saw me he changed his mind. He left half the road open. So without hesitation I sped on.

Now in Ireland, as in England, vehicles are driven on the left side of the road. This may have come down from the days of tilting or of sword play, or from the coaching days when you wanted to have your right hand free to raise your whip in salute. In speeding on, I increased the speed a little to get by in case the driver should change his mind again. Then, just as I was about to pass him, he wrenched the wheel hard about and drove out, closing off the little space he had left me through which to pass.

CRASH! The impact of the big Mercedes removed his front wheels and unhoused his engine. We were thrown up in the air. The car mounted the fence, which was made of earth and fuchsia bushes and luckily had no telephone poles on that side. I put out my left arm to prevent my wife from being flung through the glass wind screen. As I did so, I leant upon the steering wheel and turned it too much to the left. To correct this error I turned it the other way, but because there was nothing under the front wheels it went too far. At this moment the car touched the road, bounded off it diagonally, and through the other fence. It fell into a bog and the pointed radiator was buried in the soft peat.

I was shaken, for the steering wheel got me in the midriff. I was seeing silver things moving behind my eyelids. I lost my temper too, for I put the one hundred and thirty horse-power engine into reverse, in an attempt to get the car free, and the gear box was smashed to smithereens. I crawled up the back of the car out onto the road. What did I see? Good God, what is this? The two goddesses had become alive and were standing together whispering to each other. One said to me, 'Can we be of any assistance?' I was prepared for almost anything, in the temper in which I was, but not for the two goddesses becoming alive. I stared at them. Where had I seen them before? No! the ones I knew had red caste marks on their foreheads. These slender maidens' foreheads were marked with green. Behind them a very big limousine stood. I saw that the windows were covered by little pink-tasseled shades. Where was my wife? She came from behind the limousine and pointed down the road. (Thank God, she was all right!) On either side of it one of the two red-shawled priestesses was sitting in an attitude of prayer.

Each sat at the edge of one side of the road exactly in line with the other. They were calm and composed. How did they get there? They must have flown out over our heads as the car struck the fence and came suddenly to a standstill. A few hundredweight of solid wood could have broken our necks had they not been flung clear. But they were far away from where the car stopped. Too far for even the speed of the car to fling them. And then their attitude, so orderly and composed. In Ireland they say that the inevitable never happens, the unexpected always. This was the unexpected. I let it go at that. They might have been placed there by some reverent hand, but there was hardly time. The thought will occur to you that I must have had a slight concussion of the brain, that I was still in a dream world. That would be plausible enough if I were in England, where concussion of the brain is a state of mind and the better classes are born concussed; but I was in Ireland, where the dream world is external and concussion limits the imagination. Let us explain the orderly and uninjured condition of the statues by that much-suffering word *accident*. But how did two *living* princesses reach the extreme western shelf of Europe at a point farthest away from their Indian home? And who were they?

Now comes the explanation of part of this incredible tale. Because of its good salmon fishing, the Maharajah of Narawanga, Prince Ranji Sindh, had purchased the beautiful castle of Ballinahinch, with its rivers and salmon pools. Two of his nieces were visiting him in his Irish home, driving out now and again, in strict purdah or privacy, to peep at the scenery and take the air – than which there is none softer anywhere. They had seen the goddesses thrown out, sacrilegiously as it must have seemed to them, upon a country road. Had they broken their purdah to rescue these emblems of their religion? I do not know. When I recovered my sanity I went to see what had happened to the chauffeur. He happened to be the chauffeur of Sir George Bennet, sometime Post Master General of London. He was alive and expostulating, but he couldn't expostulate the gear box back on my car.

I don't remember how we got home. In Ireland, somebody always comes along to play the Good Samaritan. I have forgotten how we parted with the Indian Princesses. I remember that I ordered the statues to be deposited in the only empty building in the village of Letterfrack, a loft over a garage which was on occasion used for a court house. I was determined not to allow these sinister sisters within miles of my home. It was not long – just after the next assize – until the judge wrote to request me to remove my statues. Things were going wrong in court. So I had them sent to a wheel-wright who had a pile of wooden sections for cart wheels in his yard. They might remain in purdah, appropriate denizens of a wood pile.

Months later when, in Dublin, an antique dealer had foisted on me a spurious teapot that was supposed to be of the time of King Charles, I bethought me of my two avenging angels behind the wood pile in Connemara. I would sell them to him. They were quite genuine, I could assure him. But this was unnecessary, for when he heard where they came from and who had given them to me, he was eager to fix a price. I sent for them. They were nowhere to be found! What had become of them? I do not know. Possibly the Maharajah, at the request of his nieces, sent a party of his numerous native retainers to spirit them away. This would be a rational ex-planation – not that one requires any rational explanation of the supernatural. As the poet Yeats used to ask, why should we always try to explain the supernatural in terms of the natural or the rational as if there were nothing supernatural in life? There is enough evidence for the existence of ghosts to hang a man in any other region than that of the supernatural. Why, because a thing is beyond our comprehension, must it be 'explained?'

What the statues were, or what curse went with them, I do not know; and I do not want to know. They say that when you talk of evil spirits you conjure them up. So let us leave it at that. But one thing may be added: when my wife met Lady Eva Forbes, the sister of the man who gave me the presents, she told her that if we knew as much about the history of those statues as she did, we would realize that we had got off very lightly indeed.

There are some things in life that cannot be explained. Thank God for them. They are the things that make life worth living. We may discount the motor accident, which might happen to any English chauffeur driving for the first time in Ireland. But the timing of the visit of the two Indian prin-cesses, and the timing of their drive with the fall of the sacred images on the country road, at a spot the farthest in Europe from India, I will describe only as AN AMAZING COINCI-DENCE.

What I experienced in one legend I lost from another. I found that you cannot do as you please west of the River Suck.

The Empty Chair

Howth, as the name would tell us if we knew the language of the Danes who founded Dublin in the year 852, is a headland, in the shape of a peninsula, which forms the northern arm of Dublin Bay. It is joined to the mainland now by a thin neck of land; but it is evident that when the castle that still guards this causeway was built, it was made an island by every tide.

The first time that I dined in Howth Castle, I noticed the empty seat beside me at the table. I thought that some expected guest was late, and would have thought of it no more had not a strange thing happened which drew my attention to the empty chair and awakened my curiosity. The butler laid a plate in front of the empty seat. He replaced it by another at every course. I thought, to say the least of it, that this was very odd indeed. But in Ireland odd things are a matter of routine. So I did not like to appear to have noticed anything strange in a hospitable house. That seat may be kept there for some member of the family whose parents refuse to consider him dead. Had I not seen elsewhere a whole room kept exactly in the order that it was in when its last beloved occupant had died? Everyone is familiar with the sentiment by which we seek to make as permanent as possible our memory of our sorrow for the dead. This may be one of those tributes to a daughter or a son. The same thing happened at lunch on my second visit. On my third visit I brought a friend, and under the shelter, as it were, of his company, I asked a question, for I could stand the ritual no longer without satisfying my curiosity as to what it was all about. This is what I was told:

About three hundred years ago there dwelt on the wild west coast of Ireland a sea queen, as wild as the Atlantic waves that break against the last outpost of the continent of Europe. Her castle stood (it still stands) on a rocky island that wards off the great breakers from her tower and from the little landing place on its eastern side. Her name was Granu Aille, which in the language of the English means Grace O'Malley. Her fame has turned her name into a symbol for the whole of Ireland, which the western poets call 'Granu Aille,' just as other poets speak of Ireland as 'Dark Rosaleen' or 'Kathleen the Daughter of Houlihan.' She lived in the days of the Spanish Armada, Queen Elizabeth of England, Shakespeare, Drake and Sir Walter Raleigh. From her castle this sea queen harassed Spanish ships that traded or raided from Spain to Galway, a city founded by English merchants on the great bay that indents the island on the west. These ships brought silks and wine from Portugal or Spain and any merchandise that the prospering citizens could afford. The city was walled, for it was the bulwark of English trading farthest from home. It stood in the unknown western wilds inhabited by fierce mountain clans, and its citizens prayed: 'From the ferocious O'Flahertys may the Lord deliver us.' They had a by-law which decreed that: 'Ne "O"ne "Mac" shall strut or swagger through the streets of Galway.' And Granu Aille belonged to the former category, for she was an O'Malley. There was many a rumor that she did not stop at boarding and sinking Spanish ships, but that even English ships were sunk 'without leaving a trace,' as the latterday pirates have it. Nevertheless she got an invitation that was enough to make any Galway citizen envious: she was invited to London to see the Queen.

It took a brave heart to accept an invitation from Elizabeth. And for an Irish piratess to take the risk was proof of a stout heart. Many an Irish chief was invited to court, and ended in the Tower. But Spain was a menace, and Granu Aille had a fleet that had encountered, if her tale was true, many a tall vessel; had plundered the separated and storm-driven ships of the Great Armada as it was divided and lost around the coasts of Ireland and Scotland. Evidently she was in full favor, for the time being anyway. The story goes that Elizabeth received her well and even presented her with a handkerchief, which was declined by the sea queen for reasons of good taste and even of health. 'We are not accustomed to carry that about with us in Ireland,' she is quoted as retorting to the Queen.

It was on her return from London that the events happened which led to the custom of the empty chair. In those days Howth, on the east coast, was the nearest point to the English mainland, as indeed it is to-day; but although it was the nearest point, the nearest point on the other side was not much use to the mariner coming from Ireland to England. For it was on the island of Anglesey, which was not then connected to England proper by a bridge over the Menai Straits. Granu Aille would have to sail to Chester. This sail to Chester was known to have taken days, in adverse weather. That was why the Lords of Howth kept a special galley of twelve oars – so as to be independent of the wind, and in order to get the ear of the Queen first, before she got an 'official' version of their stewardship. It is to this that the Gaisford St Lawrence family is said to owe its survival. Communications meant a lot in those days, when a rumor was often deadlier than an official report to the ears of the Queen. And the swift-rowing galley of Howth kept not only its owner's castle, but his head upon his shoulders.

But to those coming from England to Ireland the nearest point of Ireland was of use. There was a sheltered sandy beach on the north side of Howth, just under the castle wall. One morning a strange fleet stood off the shore and strange men rowed in. In the leading boat was the stately figure of a woman seated at the stern. She had some womenfolk with her. It was Granu Aille, on her way back from London and on her way around the north coast to her western stronghold. After such a journey as that from England, the first thing you might expect on your return to your native land was a hospitable reception. Anyone who had Irish blood in his veins would have thought so; but not so the Earl of Howth. The 'mere' Irish had a way of getting people into trouble, and of getting into trouble themselves. One day they were in possession of a Queen's Pardon, the next they were being hanged, drawn and quartered. One day they were being commended for keeping the English settlers in Ireland loyal to the Throne, the next day they and the English settlers were being hunted into the hills by the Queen's Irish and English troopers, while their estates were confiscated. Even a visitor to Ireland did not always escape from the reports sent in by God knows whom to the virago Queen. Take Essex for example. He was the Queen's love; and true to breed, the Queen had his head hacked off.

The Earl of Howth looked from his battlements and saw the Sea Queen leap dry-shod ashore. Others carried her women from the boat. Her retinue of more than one hundred men formed behind her. What wild men they looked with their embroidered purple cloaks and their battle axes, the polished or gilded thongs that bound their trews to their calves, their fierce mustaches, and the fringes that almost hid their eyes!

Granu Aille! What other woman in Ireland had an army and a fleet? It was Granu Aille. Howth had heard how she had almost insulted Elizabeth by her pride and the disdainful strut of her retainers through the London streets. She may be in favor now; but the favor of the Queen to anyone in Ireland might well be a forerunner of his fate. What was it he had heard lately? Yes. There were rumors coming in from Galway that the wreckage of English ships was being found more frequently than of old in Galway Bay. If Granu Aille could not keep her retainers from acts of piracy while she was actually in the royal presence, what hope had she of disciplining them now that she had been received by the Queen? The Earl of Howth, the descendant of Sir Tristram St Lawrence, gave orders to drop the portcullis, and to close the other gates as well. He would not be 'at home' to Granu Aille.

The Sea Queen approached the castle. The outer gates were closed. Her herald blew his trumpet. There was no response from within. The Earl had forgotten that his flag was flying, showing that he was at home. When his incivility could be no longer mistaken, great indignation seized Granu Aille. Who ever heard of anyone refusing hospitality to one that was not a foe? Why, the poorest peasant would give his last bowl of milk to a stranger while his hungry children looked on. The Prince of West Connaught, the O'Flaherty, for all that he was ferocious, had a name that was synonymous with hospitable profusion. The name had come to mean all that was becoming to a prince. She herself would lodge in one of her castles on the mainland anyone who ventured to the edge of the Western Ocean. Here was a churl turning her away in front of her retainers, she that came of a stock centuries older than his. She vowed vengeance, but there was little she or her men could do. She was at peace with the English. In addition to that, the castle walls were very strong.

The little heir to the earldom of Howth was playing on the sands. He was attracted by the strange ships he saw. He had seen many ships, but none so strange as these that were built for the blue sea deep. They had no oars, but they had stout masts and spars. He liked their gaily colored sails. Suddenly he felt himself caught up and clasped to a woman's breast. That was the way his nurse used to carry him home when it was time for his noonday sleep. But this woman was not his nurse. She was taller and had a swing to her stride, and the cloak with

130

which she covered him was soft and smooth. The Earl had not known, when he shut his gates in such haste, that his only son was outside them.

The little boy did not cry. He was promised a sail in the biggest of the ships. When he reached it he was pulled up by laughing men with willing hands. The horsemen from the castle were forced to draw rein at the water's edge as the great sails bellied out to sea.

Within the castle reigned consternation and despair. What would the Sea Queen do to the son and heir of a man who had insulted her, nay, shamed her before her retinue? And all the ships that could have scattered the Great Armada might themselves become scattered and lost along the shark-toothed coast, where many a lofty ship went down. Rescue within a reasonable time was impossible. Meanwhile what would become of the child? Next day, at dawn, the sharp-eyed sentry on the castle leads sighted Granu Aille's fleet cruising beyond the Island of Lambay, which is some twelve sea miles north of Howth. News was shouted to the men within. The Earl himself ascended to the roof, for there was but little sleep for anyone within the walls that night. He could see the long ships clearly, now that the light strengthened in the east. There they sailed like swans afloat; which of them held his little son?

For fully an hour the family, and such of the garrison as were privileged, kept their eyes on the approaching vessels. They were in line now and heading south. Was it a mere ruse to tantalize the distracted parents? Rough as the men of those days were, parental love was unabated. The Earl could hardly keep his feelings concealed, even before the soldiery. One, the leading ship, was heading for the landing place. Would the weather hold? He gazed anxiously at the sky. What is that? A ship's long boat. It is rowing towards the castle and the pier. He asked the watch who had first sighted the fleet, but the boat did not contain a little boy. A herald stood with his tabard gleaming. From the boat he jumped ashore and slowly approached the castle walls. This time the gates were opened wide. But he refused to enter either courtyard or castle. Oyez! Hear the terms of Granu Aille. The child will be restored unharmed on one condition. Anxiously the Earl listened to the condition. Would the preamble never end?

'And forever for an O'Maille shall the gates be left open.

And forever for an O'Maille shall there be a place at table, until the line of the O'Mailles or the world shall end.'

Rapturously did the Earl receive the mandate. He swore by all that was held sacred, and he would ratify the oath on the tomb of Strongbow by noon. The herald returned, bringing with him the Sea Queen, her captive and her retinue. They were this time sumptuously entertained.

You will find the table set in front of the empty seat that waits for a descendant of Granu Aille to claim the hospitality that the forebears of the present holders of Howth Castle swore to give; but you will not find the great outer gates open. The reason is this: the castle grounds contain one of the loveliest hanging gardens of rhododendrons in Europe. It is on the north side of the Hill, and it ascends shelf by shelf half way up the mountain which is 560 feet high. Visitors from the city are admitted on a certain day in the week. Doubtless, when an O'Malley does appear, he or she can enter by the wicket beside the gate. One thing is certain: within the castle itself there is a place waiting for such a visitor at every meal.

Can You Shoot in a Bow?

Every boy is Robin Hood at one time or another. I was; and when I grew up I spent a lot of time reading all that there was about that personification of resistance to oppression, that lover of liberty called Robert Fitz Owd or Hood.

In the 'good green wood' the revolt against authority extended to the Church. The leaves never fall from that forest where all is youthful and beyond the law. And the bow twangs through it all.

Next, I took to shooting in a bow. I studied the history of archery about which, in England, there were more laws than about any other activity. Every barrel of wine from Spain had to pay duty into England with thirteen staves of Spanish yew. Towns had to turn out on holidays to shoot at the butts. Even to this day there is an unrepealed law which orders the students of the University of Oxford to shoot in a bow at the butts in High Street every Friday. It is an order of the Vice-Chancellor (if I remember rightly). But in my time the Vice-Chancellor had lost the power of realizing the importance of the artillery that won Agincourt, and refused to permit me, with a little group of other devotees of the bow, clad in Lincoln green, to divert the buses in order to 'shoot at the butts.'

Archery is the one exercise I have seen men practicing with creditable performance far into advanced years. There was a member of the Archery Club at Bristol who shot until he was a hundred. So, if anyone wishes to outstay his welcome in this revolving hotel of ours, let him take up archery. It promotes longevity. It has another use which I never would have attributed to it had I been left without guidance. I have the authority of no less a worthy than Bishop Hugh Latimer for the good effect of archery on morals. He also, in a sermon which he preached before the court of Henry VIII, gives an interesting account of how he learned to shoot, and from his description of it you will see how the term 'shoot *in* a bow' arose. It arose because the archer puts his body in it as the Bishop recommends. Listen to the Bishop and his praise of the bow:

133

The arte of shutyng hath bene in tymes past much estemed in this realme, it is a gyfte of Godde that he hath gyven us to excel all other nacions wythall. It hath bene Godde's instrumente, whereby he hath gyven us manye victories agaynste oure enemyes. But nowe we have taken up whoryng in tounes, instede of shutyng in the fyeldes. A wonderous thynge, that so excellente a gyfte of Godde shoulde be so lythle estemed. I desyer you, my Lordes, even as ye love the honoure and glorie of Godde, and entende to remove his indignacion, let ther be sente fourth some proclimacion, some sharpe proclimacion, to the justices of the peace, for they do not theyr dutye. Justices nowe be no justices ther be manye goode actes mayde for thys matter alreadye. Charge them upon theyr allegiaunce that thys syngulare benefyte of Godde maye be practysed and that it be not turned into bollyng, glossyng and whoryng wythin the tounes, for they be negligente in executyng these lawes of shutyng.

In my tyme my poore father was as diligente to teach me to shute as to learne anye other thynge, and so I thynke other menne dyd theyr children. He taught me howe to drawe, howe to laye my bodye in my bowe, and not to drawe wyth strengthe of armes, as other nacions do, but wyth strengthe of the bodye. I had my bowes boughte me accordyng to my age & strengthe; as I encreased in them, so my bowes were made bygger and bygger, for menne shall never shute welle, excepte they be brought up in it. It is a goodely arte, a holsome kynde of exercyse, much commended in physike. Marsilius Ficinus, in hys boke *de triplici vita* (it is a greate whyle sins I red hym nowe), but I remembre he commendeth thys kynde of excercyse, and sayeth that it wrestleth agaynste manye kyndes of diseases. In the reverence of God, lete it be contynued.

When you join a club devoted to a sport with a tradition as old as the tradition of archery, there are many delightful discoveries to be made. The first is that such a club is a reservoir of tips and practices handed down by word of mouth, and not to be found in books. It is the guardian of the tradition of the sport. Then there is the discovery of the bowyer to be made, a man with some old serviceable name like Inderwick or Isserman, men whose forebears have done nothing but make bows, first for 'the yeomen, the bowmen,' and then for 'the nobility and gentry' when archery was continued as a sport. You will learn how an archery meeting is conducted, and get an insight into the formality of English sport, its ritual, its observances.

Your time must be your own. That is the way certain clubs in England maintain their exclusiveness; only people of independent means can join. They rarely if ever meet on the popular Saturdays, but rather on Wednesdays and Thursdays. There is (or at least there was before the war) at the core of the Royal Toxophilite Society, an inner circle of rich men who invite a dozen or so of like station to their country houses for an archery week. This was done turn-about and was so *de rigueur* that one of the group whom I knew, on being ordered abroad for his health, left his house open and appointed a deputy to entertain the archers while he was away. It was his turn!

It is a jolly sight to see the red, blue, white and gold targets facing each other in a closely-shorn field. Three or four at each end at, for the commencement, sixty yards apart. The distance is marked with whitewash by a line a yard in front of the target. While a member advances to shoot, the others remain behind the target and preserve a formal silence. There are six-dozen arrows to be shot at sixty yards, four at eighty and two at a hundred-yard range. Twelve dozen in all. This is the York Round. Three arrows at a time are shot by each competitor, then all change ends. Thus a good and gradual walk can be covered during the course of the day, and, if your bow is, say, a fifty pounder, that is, one that requires a pull equal to fifty pounds to stretch it to the arrow head, you shall have pulled some tons' weight before the day is over. And all this is a graduated and non-violent exercise. I do not know whether to attribute longevity to this exercise, or to the freedom from care which the members, of independent and carefree means, enjoy.

It is an interesting thing to visit a master of any handicraft in this age of mass and non-human production. It does one good to see a mastercraftsman working with his hands. Such a man was the bowmaker or bowyer in Slazenger's, the sports store in London. He would choose his stave of Spanish yew and make you a bow to order. The stave comes from the female yew by choice and the advantage of the yew is that its 'cast' is softer, without being one whit less forceful, than bows of a sharper and more sudden cast. A good self-yew, that is an unspliced or unbacked bow, costs the equivalent of sixty to eighty dollars.

The traditional way to shoot in England is this: the archer stands with his left side facing the target; his feet are at right angles to it and about a foot apart, far enough to give him a good balance, for he is about to turn himself into a gun carriage. He holds the bow horizontally while he lays the arrow with the cock feather up on the little mother-of-pearl mark above the grip. He pulls the arrow back and notches it. The cock feather shows that the other two feathers are lying flat. He then raises his arm and stretches it to full length with his wrist turned very slightly in, draws back the string which he holds in three fingers, the upper two having the arrow between them, pulls it back to the angle of his jaw and 'looses' it. The loosing must be done cleanly and sharply and is a knack that must be learned on the field. If it is done in a slovenly manner, the fingers will open and shorten the expansion of the bow and let the arrow project too far. In effect, weaken and spoil the shot. As for the grip on the bow, I have seen men carry their bows with their grip unrelaxed all day, once they 'got it.'

At sixty yards the bow is too strong, so one does not aim directly at the target, but aims the arrow head below it at some spot or tuft in the grass about half way between the archer and the target. You cannot aim along an arrow; aiming is therefore indirect and depends on practice and co-ordination more than on sighting. At eighty yards you may aim on the target, at one hundred at an imaginary point about ten yards above it – depending on the strength of one's bow.

In the field, the difference in the American practice of shooting, compared with the English, appears. The American archer aims directly. This possibly explains how America has managed to excel so far in archery that 'nacion gyfted by Godde to excel all other nacions wythall.' Its figures for the York Round are beyond any records in England. The American archer stands easily, not necessarily at right angles to the target. He draws the bow string in a line with his nose and chin, and not, as in England, to his ear. This enables him to see directly along the arrow at which he looks past the left side of the bow string. This is 'drawyng wyth the strengthe of armes as other nacions do' with a vengeance. The body is not laid in the bow, and, as a result, it is not possible to use as strong a bow if you are shooting after the American fashion. The bow is grasped loosely so that the knuckles are not blanched. Compare this with the grip that some archers maintain during a match in England for hours on end, once their hand begins to fit the bow. Then a bright metal peg is permitted to give the point of aim at distances under eighty yards.

There is in Death Valley, Colorado, an archer who can shoot an arrow five hundred yards from his shoulder and eight hundred when the bow is fixed to his feet. This incredible distance is due largely to the improvement in bow and arrow making and to a knowledge of ballistics which the merrie men had not.

The best bowyer, probably the greatest archer-craftsman in the world, lives near Port Washington on Long Island. He makes bows in the American fashion – flat like the spring of a car. His yew comes from the mountain forests of Washington, from an elevation of five thousand feet, and, as in England, the female yew is chosen by the forest rangers, who mark a likely branch, cut it, and after seven years of seasoning, send the staves to him.

He splices them with a fishtail splice hidden beneath the handle, polishes and pares the wood until the required shape and strength are reached. Then he makes notches in the wood at both ends for the bow string; but does not use the deer's horn as they do in England. When you think of the precious wood and the time and the difficulty of obtaining it, the cost of a bow does not exceed the cost of an English bow and is not dear. The arrows are more hard to come by. The right wing of an eagle is used. In England, the feathers of a peacock were considered best, though the archers who fought in France and Scotland had to be content with a grey goose wing. The choice of the feathers of a particular bird and wing is not fanciful. It has to do with the torque or turning of the arrow in its flight.

This 'holsome kynde of exercyse' was 'much commended in physike' four hundred years ago, when the world was comparatively easy-going. It is commendable now, for it can, such as no other exercise, improve the figure of young women, and cause men to stand straight, and flat-shouldered. With all the noise, clatter and confusion of the present day, it is more commendable than ever for the young, for its history will fill them with brave and generous sentiments. It is not nearly so expensive as golf and it has a tradition and romance which golf has not. To those who can idle in the 'grene shaw' the freedom and the old world merriment of the forest will come again. There is no more soothing and soft sound than the twang of a bow, nor a more satisfactory one than that of 'the clap in the clout' as the arrow strikes the target.

Archery, which can enormously strengthen the back muscles, is excellent for those who want to improve the contour of the breast. What have the muscles of the back to do with the breasts? Nothing, if they are allowed to become flaccid, and disused; but everything if they are strengthened to a point where they can pull the shoulders back until the bosom is broadened, and the position of the breasts raised into correct posture.

If archery were made, not a compulsory course, for nothing good comes from compulsion, but a course at the disposal of all growing girls in schools and colleges, we would see a more stately and upstanding race. There are hundreds of archery clubs all over the country, but the practice of archery, shooting in a bow, should begin as early as Bishop Latimer's did – in childhood. I recommend a hundred arrows a day – to make Dianas.

The Nine Naked Arabs

If you look along the Liffey to the West in the evening, you will see many spires and minarets rising through the smoke against an angry sky; and one dark tower that tapers somewhat to be crowned by a bulbous dome or cupola. This, under its smoke, is the great Brewery founded by Arthur Guinness of the Eighty Acres. And the dark tower is the tower of the malt-house of what is Dublin's pride and part of Ireland's solution of the problem of Life, for, between sporting and drinking the best of brews, Ireland has made its pleasures pay for its shortcomings: by betting on the horse races you can help to maintain a hospital; and by ordering a Guinness you may drink a soul out of a slum, for slum-clearing was a philanthropy of one of the owners of the great Brewery.

You can lean on the bridge and gaze upon this strange and wistful scene as long as you like. No one will interfere, not even a policeman, for leisure is the prerogative of the town. Probably you will be joined by some citizen unoccupied for the moment by petty concerns and duties, who will follow your eye and utter a word of sad praise with the gentle melancholy that is so becoming to philosophy, some little affirmation beginning with 'Aye; indeed.'

I leant and pondered lately, looking at my swans which have increased in numbers, thanks to the malt that mingles with the water, gazing over their heads and over the bridges that span the stream. My eyes fell from the topless towers hidden in the evening glow, and looked along the quayside when they beheld forty Chinamen coming out of the East. They gazed no more that way.

Startled, I went off immediately to take counsel with Brinsley Macnamara because I knew that he could be relied on to interpret this unusual thing. I told him of the apparition of the Forty Chinamen.

'Yes,' he said, somewhat nonchalantly as I thought. 'They came off a tanker. Did you not read the *Irish Times* this morning? I hope that they are not going to be as devout as the nine Arabs who visited this city some years ago.'

'Nine Arabs?'

'Yes. Nine Naked Arabs. Everyone in the town knows about them. I am surprised that you have not heard of them. Where have you been? They are legendary now.'

He was right. I had been away. I had seen much and gained much experience; but then, look at what I had missed, nine naked Arabs! My Chinamen were clothed.

'Shape me the city's legend,' I implored.

He began in his precise way, smiling at the tale as he unfolded it.

'Years ago nine Arabs got off a boat one evening somewhere along the quays. They wandered past the Custom House where the lighters were loading barrels. They did not know a word of English but they listened attentively to what they heard. The only word they heard was 'Guinness.' Wherever they went; at every corner the refrain was the same: 'Mine's a pint of Guinness,' 'Make mine a Guinness,' or 'A Guinness, if you don't mind.' They thought that 'Guinness' was not a word but the name of the King of the Country or there was a god of the place and that Guinness was his prophet. They were confirmed in this conclusion by a lady who went by spinning like a dancing dervish and asservating loudly that Guinness was good.'

'But,' I interposed, 'did they not know that there is no King in Ireland. It is a republic according to the Sublime Poste and the Encyclopaedia Britannica.'

'Well, they thought it was the name of its Prophet, and they could understand the worship of a Prophet and, being devout, they sought the local Mecca.'

Here I refrained from trying a pun by saying, 'And the Mecca of the locals,' not because I am learning to curb my style, but because it would interfere with the course of the narrative; and Brinsley is the best story-teller we have left.

'They progressed along half a dozen quays and past four or five bridges when they came to the pier where perspiring men with three mystic letters on their breasts were loading Guinness and trundling barrels marked with the name. They bowed towards each other first and then towards the brewery from the corner of which a tall, almost Arabian figure emerged. With great courtesy he inquired if he could help them in any way for to him it was obvious that they had come to the wrong

140

side of the brewery which they wished to visit. Visitors are admitted at the Jame's Gate side. 'Guinness?' he inquired. They bowed. They had learned the name now. 'Guinness,' they replied. With his walking stick he directed them somewhat profusely, but no more profusely than the manner in which he was thanked. It is a pity that they could not grasp his explanation of the name. '"Originally Mag Inis,"' he said. '"Mag a plain; Inis an island. This, for instance, is Usher's Island. The 'Island Plain' is up in the North; Mag Guinness; But you can get Guinness plain here."' His thick moustache hid his smile. At the name they inclined their heads again. He pointed with his stick toward Robert Street and swept it sideways with a jerk to indicate the turn they should take to reach the reception room. He gave it a little twitch to indicate that they should hurry, for already it was late. In their white burnouses they moved silently along the dark, windowless walls of the street. Again they heard the name for the street urchins shouted "They are going to Guinnesses!"

'As they went along, the smell of barm grew stronger. They were on the right track. From some lighted houses they could hear the word Guinness repeated many times. What fervor! Almost as holy as Mecca is the town! They turned to the right; but the great doors of the mosque were closed. It was after sunset. They settled themselves to pray. First they knelt for a moment; now the voice of the muezzin from one of the minarets would be heard. Behind them, across the street, they heard a crowd repeating the name. Without turning they touched the pavement with their foreheads. Still no voice or sound. As night fell they divested themselves of their clothes and bending forward rested their foreheads on the ground. All through the night they remained so. Soon the sun would catch the tower. The voice would call the Faithful to prayer. The gates would swing wide. In this hope they remained wrapt. Meanwhile the moon was looking down with a cold indifferent eye, the moon that watches nations and tribes in their appropriate places and has regarded unemotionally through the centuries many diverting sights. Gently its light fell on the helmet of a policeman and made it gleam faintly, for the helmet was dark. Dark, too, were nine naked posteriors pointed upwards towards the moon. For a moment the guardian of the law surveyed the scene. He had seen people at prayer before, but they were not so absorbed as to refuse to answer questions.

141

It was indecent exposure at any rate. He raised his baton nine times and brought it down nine times in succession as he went down the file of those who worshipped and waited.'

I covered my eyes. 'Stop, stop! I cannot bear it,' I exclaimed, shocked at the picture Brinsley conjured up. 'What must they have thought of Guinness?'

'It served them right. They were teetotatllers.' That gentle philosophizing mood which comes over me at times ever since I met AE, came over me now.

'Doubtless they saw in the policeman the Wrath of the Prophet personified, for it may have dawned upon them at last that Guinness was a drink. But I cannot see how the outrage can be condoned.'

'Perhaps in the Pleroma, in the Fullness of Things, where all things meet and are resolved,' Brinsley said sardonically. 'The apparent discrepancy between a bowed forehead bent in prayer and a whack on the beam-end may be explained: "I am the Kisser and the Kiss. I am the Slayer and the Slain." But while they were on their pilgrimage in Dublin it must have been hard to understand.'

USA

Noise

I was standing under the Elevated in Third Avenue trying to make myself a good citizen for the time being by accustoming myself to noise. I thought that I was standing in a becoming pose like Dionysus listening to Echo, close to a pillar, yet a truck driver blew his horn to correct my stance as it were. A bus stopped right in front of me, opened one of its doors with a hissing sound and disgorged a few passengers. I was in their way. I moved back. A loud warning and a squealing of brakes hailed me. I stepped forward again. The bus driver despaired of me as a passenger for he closed his door with a bang and, with a snort of compressed air, was gone. I looked for the lights but they are not easily seen when you are right under the Elevated. There was a moment's lull in the traffic. I thought that I would chance a crossing when suddenly a train roared with an iron clangor overhead. This so confused me that I couldn't hear the remarks of a taxi driver who was under the impression that he had just saved my life and was spurning all hope of emolument. The awful roar above increased with my confusion. It was driving home the last krieg against the 'elected' silence in my ears. It had won out by noise. What was I to do? I held the pillar and began to cogitate like Socrates in the open street. I contemplated the pillar which though unelaborately designed was not truly Doric. While noticing this I lost my chance of crossing while the momentary lights favored me. I will never become a good citizen if I cannot get a move on. That was evident. But how could I who could not stand the sounds of progress of the elevated expect to become a good citizen? I have it! Go upstairs, buy a ticket and become a co-partner of the clamor: become a 'Big Noise' yourself by moving to the sounds of the Age of Iron. Rush up and down the City of New York, crashing along in the Elevated – advance with its deadly diapason into all the windows of the stricken houses on either side. Rattle the doors and shake the rust off the fire-escapes. Shock the children into slumber so that they may be as civilized as the London children who got a neurosis from the

145

stillness when they were evacuated to the countryside. Let others hear the noise of which you have become a part. You are now a thunderbolt riding the astounded air, an envy of all the meaner mortals with pneumatic drills below. Do not dismount until the streets become narrower, that's where Echo loves to dwell. Wait until the stations change the symphony in which you are as yet unable to recognize the subtler roars. Get off if possible near a hospital if you want to hear what noise can be and how far your alien ears are from the full realization of what fractured air can do.

I did not get off at a hospital. But I got off at a quiet place where there was no traffic comparable to that of the middle town. I could walk if I had courage and if my balancing apparatus had not shared in the concussion of labyrinthine ears. Suddenly the most appalling shrieks and wailings rent the air. I thought I had heard all the noises. I thought I had achieved the bliss of tone deafness when this appalling agony of sound wailed near. No human torture could produce that audible despair, I knew. What are they torturing? And is it escaping in this direction more agonized and anguished than all the unacclimatized souls in Hell? A sabre-tooth tiger interrupted on his honeymoon by a mastodon treading inadvertently on its tail could not rival the spiral shrieks that ascended into the air. I sought refuge in flight.

As I went scurrying along the sidewalk a bell rang and from a trap-door in the ground a man rose slowly from the underworld. Noise had wakened the dead. I was not surprised.

As he ascended into the light of day a bell rang, as if it were a slow-motion rehearsal in the Fire Department; but behind me the primordial menagerie was coming closer on scream.

I swerved into a saloon for sanctuary. The wailing followed me in. If this is America's version of the Banshee, we have not a leg to stand on in Ireland when it comes to the supernatural.

I leant upon a table that two people had just left. Under its glass top it burst into sound and flame. A little ball began to jingle under the glass as it hopped from electric light to light. A legend assured the beholder that hell was a-poppin'. I have heard of table rapping but here was a table jingling of its own accord. The Banshee wailed outside. I looked towards the bartender. I wondered if he heard it, or was it heard only by me alone? I was about to ask him when, over his head, a radio roared a question at me:

'Have you pre-soaked?'

Faintly I beckoned a waiter. It was useless to hail him. No one could hear amid the din.

'Did you hear it?' I asked.

'It's only one of those soap advertisements. Forget it.'

'Not that. Not that,' I said. 'But the wailing sounds that just swept by.'

He looked blank. So it was for my ears alone the wailing was. I bowed the doomed head. Just then a little bell rang in the table. I had forgotten the horse races that were going on under the glass.

As I thought it over I began to realize that if the Banshee followed me to New York she would have to step up the wails that portend death otherwise she would be inaudible. Strange that no one else seems to have heard her. Outside the wailing died away. I looked out. An ambulance was standing by a wall marked:

QUIET PLEASE

It's not a banshee but a siren that acts as a banshee when some poor citizen is being borne to hospital. For him, if he be an Irishman of family sufficiently ancient, a banshee will keen at the approach of death. I could give many instances of Fairyland making itself manifest in broad daylight in Ireland; but people are inclined to discount the Old Sod as being too full of fairies for practical purposes. They are more influenced by England. So I must recount any vestiges of the supernatural I can think of in that pedestrian country which has lost the fairy faith. Here are some English supernatural noises:

1. Noises are said to be heard beneath the Long Barrow called Fairy Toot in Somerset.
2. Beautiful music comes from a barrow at Sidwell Fields, Quantock Hills, at night time.

A barrow is, of course, a burial mound. These sounds are not very satisfactory except that they prove that Fairyland sounds in England yet, though its sounds are not necessarily heard by day. But what are we to make of this?

3. Music is also said to be heard at midday at the apex of Music Barrow at Culliford Tree, Bincombe Downs, Dorset.

At midday! And you have the address in full if you want to hear music for yourself. For me there is music enough in the names alone: Bincombe Downs and Culliford Tree.

My contention or my submission, rather, is very simple. It is this: if the fairies can be heard at midday at the apex of Music Barrow, Bincombe, why not at the end of Third Avenue? What is wrong with New York that the 'sweet everlasting voices' should be still? He who has an ear let him hear. As for me I am convinced. Have I not listened? Have I not overheard? Perhaps it is this quest that gave rise to the citizens' habit of adjuring each other to 'Lissen!'

Some day they all will hear the fairy toot. Today New York is no place for a reverie.

'There it comes again!' I said.

'Oh, that? Only an ambulance driving some poor guy to a hospital.'

I looked and lo! an ambulance marked Hospitals Department was again acknowledging the request, 'Quiet Please,' which graced a hospital wall.

'But why that awful wail?'

'To clear traffic.'

'Even when there is no traffic? Cannot they be satisfied with a bell like the Fire Department which goes into action like a flying steeple?'

He thought that I was being merely facetious, the one thing that I never am, especially when I have had a fright. When I get out of this, I promised myself, I will ask a taxi driver. He will explain why it is that patients must go to hospital listening to their agonies turned to sound. Is it to cheer them by letting the neighbors hear their pain and so sympathize with the sound when they cannot have sight of the patient? What is the idea? It cannot be always to clear traffic and if it goes on day by day I am pretty sure that it goes on by night. This may be to soothe the overtolerant New Yorkers to sleep. Wait until I get outside and hail a cab. Then the taxi man will tell me more. Behind my thoughts lay a little layer of disappointment. Not at the fact that I wasn't going to die. Nobody, or few, want to do that. But I was disappointed that I couldn't get it over to my kinsfolk here in the States, so that they in future generations might boast:

'We have a siren for a Banshee in our family.'

Everyone knows that the Banshee or White Fairy wails

outside the house at the approaching death of a member of the family. But it is only the oldest families that have a Banshee. It would set us up no end here if we could put it over that the Banshee turned into a siren when we came to the United States because there was so much noise that the voice of the unearthly visitant was liable to pass unnoticed. It would be merely an adjustment to environment and not one bit more extraordinary than the Three Enchanted Chimneys which appear, to me at least, every night when I look over the East River.

I hailed a talking taxi man.

'Why must they make such hideous noises with sirens when a patient is being taken to hospital?'

'To warn traffic.'

'But won't a bell do such as the Fire Department uses?'

'With the windows shut on a cold night a driver might not hear a bell. So they figure that the siren is the best thing to hear. The Mayor uses one.'

That left me aghast. The Mayor of all people. The Mayor who started an Anti-Noise campaign and ended by making noon hideous with prolonged blasts every Saturday. And now he has a siren on his car.

'The Mayor,' I queried, 'Why does he want to go about like a disease?' But the question was too strong for my informant. So:

'Tell me. Does this kind of thing play at night?'

'Sure.'

'But the streets are comparatively empty and people want some sleep even in New York.'

'It seems to sound more at night.'

He was defending it! Of course it sounds louder because it has less noise to drown. It would be unnecessary if there were civilized silence in the city.

'It seems to sound more at night.' I thought of the Nachtlied:

Night it is. Now sound louder all singing springs; and my heart is a singing spring.

I had an idea.

'Drive me to the first restaurant that has no door porter.' The idea was that if there were no door porter there would very likely be no 'Entertainer' to give the guests peptic ulcers. But I was wrong. The money saved on a door porter was expended on an entertainer. I had imagined that I could eat in peace and

149

enjoy in silence the few thoughts that use my brain as an unfurnished apartment when they find themselves far from home. I have not a bad conscience so it will not be necessary to put a dime in the juke box to drive all thought away.

The place was small and clean and packed. It had a girl dressed as a boy carrying a small piano on her stomach and moaning through her nose. She was rendered almost inaudible by a shriek of jazz which came from an illuminated coal scuttle and by a waiter who kept irregular counterpoint by avalanching all the knives and forks he could collect. Chairs moved on the floor. The juke box stopped. Some fellow with an empty mind that had to be filled with noise dropped a coin into it and turned away without listening. Guests roared at each other over the tables.

Until the public realizes that you can become prone to cancer as a result of the constant shock to the nervous system caused by unceasing noise and tension, there will be no peace in the big cities. Alexis Carroll has spoken to the same purpose. Statistics showing the relation of noise to cancer might accomplish something.

When they find out that the noisiest cities have the most cases of cancer they will take the sirens off the ambulances. Meanwhile the cancerous sounds go on.

I envied a fellow with a little black earphone stuck to the side of his skull. He had got to 'where beyond these voices there is peace.' He could turn his hearing on and off. Mostly off, I should imagine, for what on earth is there to hear? He was luckily unaware of the shouts of the diners who, driven to making themselves heard above the unceasing din, had achieved a deadly audibility that turned anyone within thirty feet into an eavesdropper.

Now there are some cheering and brave noises which are grand to hear. For my part I like the sound of a moss-born brook when it finds its first stone and gurgles like a baby laughing. And the sounds of the bursting furze pods in the August heat; and the song of the black bird of Letter Lee. After that the splash from the water wheel of an old mill. I like the thunder which breaks out when the engines of an air ship are opening up and we are climbing air; or the brave noises of a river boat that no one resents. I like the seething sound when a yacht heels over on a tack. The ring of a skate on the ice; the thunder on the turf when the horses are entering the straight –

and this, the merriest noise I ever heard, the laughter of a lot of young girls in a lecture room. I never liked the sound of wind. It means a change of weather or some unsettling thing, probably for the worst.

What sound did Oliver Basselin like? The sound of a cooper hammering on a barrel.

'Ho, the bonnie noise! Soon there will be drinking.'

It is surprising that height does not save you from the noise of New York. Comfortably housed on a thirty-fourth story I could hear the street noises as if they were on the same level as the window sill. I have been told the explanation; but that does not alter the fact that there is no escape. Not even if you flew at 14 miles a minute, which is beyond the speed of sound, you could not fly away from people who emanate noises as mechanically and as brainlessly as a katydid.

It is a long call from the oaf with the nickel for the juke box to the tramp of Kylemore Pass in Connemara who said to a friend of mine as he passed her home:

'It's a fine still place you have here, Ma'am. God bless it.'

Don't Go Mad in Manhattan

The telephone rang at 11:30 precisely. The owner of the voice was in the habit of going to bed at ten o'clock. To hear from her at this hour was remarkable, so I noted the time.

'Are you dressed? Then come round at once. It is urgent. I will tell you all when you arrive.'

That excited, startled whisper! My mind was full of conjectures. What could it be? Bad news from the front? Thieves locking her into her bedroom? Her apartment was only round the corner. I had no time to sort my guesses before I arrived.

Her butler was in hospital. She opened the door herself. She was alone with the cook in the apartment. I never saw anyone more agitated and alarmed within the confines of reason. She beckoned me into the living room. Her finger was at her lips. She whispered pointing to the kitchen which was beyond the hall. The door was closed with a key remaining in the lock.

'Elka's in there. I think that she has gone mad. She says that she can see you looking out of your window and listening to a woman's screams who has been calling all day and yet she will not open her door or let anyone in to help her. She is having a baby; and no one can get in.'

'How can she see me?' I began. Then realizing the futility of discussing the theme of madness, 'I will speak to her,' I said.

'Oh, I wish you would.'

I unlocked the door of the kitchen. There was no one there. I knocked on the door of the bedroom adjoining. I heard a stir. 'May I come in?' I inquired. Fearing that she might be preparing to jump from the window at my approach or that she might lock the door, I opened it and looked in.

'I am here, Elka. Can I help?'

She turned a face devoid of spirit slowly towards me as I spoke. She raised a hand signalling silence.

'There it is again,' she said.

'What is it?' I asked.

'The poor woman that is having the baby. She has locked herself in. No one can help her. Listen!'

There was nothing to which to listen except street noises and they were abundant. I thought it best to humor her. Why is it everyone tries to appease a mad person? There is little left to humor. Reason is gone and they are far away.

'Stay there and listen carefully until I come back.'

Outside I found her mistress more agitated if possible than before. There is something awful in the presence of a human being possessed by a spirit that is distraught. It is worse than the fear of ghosts. A ghost is at work in flesh and blood.

'We must get a doctor at once who will certify her. She must be cared for in a neurological clinic. You cannot have her with you all night in the apartment with no help.'

I got in touch with a medical friend though it was close to midnight. He came without delay. We explained the circumstances as well as we could. He went at once to the cook's bedroom. He was out in a moment. He did not speak but he turned his closed hand significantly. Lock her up, it meant.

'The first thing to do,' he whispered, 'is to get the next of kin. They must be notified without delay.'

The next of kin turned out to be a sister. She took the message rather stoically, the doctor remarked.

Now red tape began to unwind.

It is not permissible to send a patient who has become insane to Bellevue in a taxi. Too many irresponsible persons might make too many diagnoses at the expense of their friends. Bellevue instructed us in the proper procedure. The first thing to do is to find a policeman. Ask him to call Bellevue and request them to send their ambulance for the patient.

It is not easy to find a cop after midnight in Park Avenue. This is a tribute to the probity of Park Avenue and to the parsimony of the Mayor. At last the doctor found a policeman some eight or nine blocks away. He obligingly came to the apartment and telephoned to his station which telephoned to Bellevue. The hospital informed the police that owing to manpower shortage there was only one ambulance running and that was somewhere up in Harlem and would not have all that district taken care of for some hours. There were thirteen cases reported. Ours was the fourteenth.

The doctor had to return home. At one-thirty the policeman called his station again. They put the inquiry through. Had we not been informed that the only ambulance was on duty up town collecting the night's 'mentals?' We must wait our turn.

The policeman was a kind person. He had a family at Westchester. He thought it better not to see the cook. 'The uniform might frighten her.' He refused any alcoholic refreshment. We sat for another hour and a half, talking occasionally in whispers. The night was wearisome after all the excitement of the earlier part. So the two of us and a sober cop and an insane cook sat and wore out the hours of the early morning. Truly it was a dark hour before the dawn.

I asked the cop what kind were the 'mentals' of a night in up-town New York.

'Oh, half a dozen drink-crazed negroes, a few suicides and a religious case or two. They can be very cunning and lash out at you when you least expect it.'

Nice company for our cook I thought, who was over-solicitous for a woman in labor who did not exist. I wondered how we could get her into the 'Mad Truck' without a struggle. I turned over in my mind the propriety of telling lies to lunatics. I remembered the statement of Socrates as to when lies in such cases were permissible. Of the lie he thought, 'When those whom we call our friends in a fit of madness or illusion are going to do some harm, then it is useful and is a sort of medicine or preventive.'

I would tell Elka when the wagon came for her that she was going where she might help the woman in childbirth. Cryptically and cynically true.

At a quarter to three we thought we heard the ambulance. It was some large truck that had stopped near the building, scavenging department most likely. A false alarm.

The policeman told us that there had been a raid in the early hours of the preceding morning on an apartment building near by. The information came by telephone that a woman was in labor but that help could not reach her because she was shut in. Mr Fairchild (naming the manager) was the father. A name of good omen if heredity went for anything I thought. 'It sounds like our Elka,' her mistress remarked. Putting the experience required to get in touch with the police and send them on a false alarm together with the apathy of her sister on hearing the news of Elka's illness, we concluded that it was not the first time that Elka had gone off her head. But we had to be very careful in making any statements that might invalidate the earning power of the person accused. The doctor was so careful in the choice of words. 'Ill, in need of rest and hospitalization.'

154

At last something stopped again. Loud voices inquiring for all the neighborhood to hear:

'Is there a mad woman here?'

A great lump of a man entered the apartment. He nodded to the officer and said as if it were a formality 'I take over now.' He was much overweight even for his great frame. His head was small and his mouth was soft but otherwise there was nothing to suggest sympathy with his charges.

'Where is she?'

He swaggered into the room indicated. 'Come on now put on yer clothes. You don't want me to take you away like that do ye?'

I rushed in with my Socratic lie.

'Do dress yourself Elka and go to see the poor woman in labor.'

Gently Elka said, 'If you will only go out of the room, I will dress myself.'

Possibly for her safety the attendant did not go out. Elka got into her bed and began dressing under the shelter of the bed clothes. In a short space, no, it was long, drawn out as Elka's delay and the attendant's brittle patience permitted, Elka was up. She was taken unceremoniously by the arm and led away. But not to the shelter of a friendly hospital yet. During his wait while she was dressing the attendant informed us that he would have to take the cook along to Welfare Island where a case had been reported; but he thought that was the last call of the night.

So it took from 11:30 until long after 3 a.m. to get the poor demented body to the ambulance. It was, we ascertained, after five when she reached her destination.

I wondered what would have happened had the case been that of a homocidal maniac instead of a complaisant woman. There would have been time not only for us all to be killed but for rigor mortis to set in.

On the whole I think that the best place to lose your reason is *inside* an asylum, an open air one such as Dublin is my choice; but perhaps you have a capital of your own in mind.

Tea With Queen Anne

There is something very enjoyable in being all alone on your first day in a strange town. If you analyze this feeling it will resolve itself into a sense of freedom coupled with a power for opinions and to pass judgment on things, as free from appeal as if you were an invisible judge. I always enjoy wandering about without a guide and seeing places and things for myself. Houses suggest more when you don't know their history for that might be humble and insignificant. It does you little good to be informed that the magnificent castle upon the hill, turreted and towered, is only the high school or the county infirmary. Leave me free and uninformed with a town at my feet, and I will enjoy myself.

Some unkind commentator might suggest that the pleasure I thus derive is due to the fact that there are so many people who do not know me in a strange town. As a matter of fact in Charleston where I was wandering there were some people and charming ones to whom I was known and whom I was to visit at a less early hour. So I spent the time wandering and wondering and revolving the old city's history in my mind.

I love old squares and alleyways or cobbled courts with trees and dim passages with strange doors. I love old gracious streets. Charleston has many of these and old rose-red houses, too, asleep in the blinding sun.

The house I sought had no number. Houses should never have a number, that is if the owner has any personality at all. My hostess had great personality. You could see it in her house when you looked through the tall narrow gate at its windows and chimney pots which were built in the days of Queen Anne. And since then nothing has changed without or within.

'So good of you to come.' She held out her hand.

'So good of you to ask me.'

'I hear that you are dying for a cup of properly made tea. Won't you sit down?'

Light shone on the tea urn which was busily steaming on its oval tray. It shone on the tea caddy, the tea basin, the sugar bowl and the tall tea pot and on the bright silver hair of my hostess. She seemed to be dressed in blue but the movement of a lace shawl distracted the impression. She sat erect on one of those chairs on which the act of sitting is a lost accomplishment. I could never do it. I know that I would impale the back of my head on the little spires or tear the cane seat.

Duly the water went in and was poured out after it had warmed the teapot. 'It is impossible to impress on servants that they must warm the teapot,' she remarked. I looked at the servant who stood, wide-eyed, behind her chair. He seemed as interested as if he had seen the process for the first time.

'A teaspoonful for each and one for the pot,' she said smiling, as she condescended to repeat the common receipt. I felt that I had to say something by way of table talk, something about tea that would not be contentious or political. I had been warned against talking politics, particularly about the North and the South, for it seemed that the politics of those days are as contemporary in Charleston as the politics of Cromwell in Ireland. I could easily have done so for, I am glad to say, I am one of the greatest failures in politics (which is different from being the greatest political failure) anyone could hope to meet.

'In the days of Charles the Second and saturnine,' I began, 'teapots were very small so precious was the tea.'

'Naturally,' she said. This would have been disconcerting had she not held up a lump of sugar in the tongs and asked, 'Sugar?'

'No, no, no! I am too conceited for sugar. I don't wish to grow fat.' And I gave one of those well-bred little laughs that would indicate incipient tuberculosis in anyone not to the manner born.

'You were speaking of Charles the Second.'

'What made me mention him,' I said, 'is that, being unaware of the rarity of tea in his reign, I bought a large and of course spurious tea-pot from a dealer. The hall-mark had been forged with a soft metal die instead of a steel punch. The tea pot was fluted and as large as that,' I said, pointing before I realized that it was bad form to comment on the furniture.

'As for this,' she said loftily, lifting the tea-pot, 'It has been in the family for 220 years and more.'

Why I asked myself had I mentioned that dealer? Could I not have mentioned my Charles the Second pot without disparaging it? Perhaps. But everyone knows that nothing I possess lasts two hundred years.

'Do you like it strong or weak?'

'Just as it comes out of the pot.'

'Milk?'

'Please.'

She handed me my cup remarking, 'As you do not take sugar, rationing will not hurt you.'

Now, now, I said to myself, this is where politics may come in and spoil the tea party. I do not know what opinions she holds but, judging by the fearless blue eyes and the Cavalier's forehead, whatever opinions she holds, she holds fast.

I sipped the tea and said 'Delicious.' Then in order to enhance her tea by dispraising all others; I tried a little anecdote.

'Do you know that when visiting Niagara,' I began, 'I crossed over into Canada hoping that I might get some real tea.'

'And was it good?'

'Oh no. Just the same old story: tea with lingerie.' A sudden chill seemed to pervade the room. She glanced quickly and compressed her look. An awful thought struck me: Heavens, she thinks that I am referring to the undies of the waitresses and not to those abominable little tea bags. She has probably never seen the muslin of a tea bag in her life. I rushed up reinforcements:

'It is so hard to get away from those little tea bags,' I explained. She never spoke. 'Little bags,' I said again, 'you know?' Apparently she did not know. Apparently she had never travelled from tea bag to tea bag across the breadth of the land. She may never have been outside Charleston, perhaps never outside her house. Maybe she is Queen Anne!

Coldly she said, 'I am afraid that we are at cross purposes. What has lingerie to do with tea?'

Now was my chance to reinstate myself and dispel any ideas of a *double entendre*.

'Tea is served in the majority of restaurants all over the USA in little muslin tea bags which are lowered into the pot, or, more shockingly, placed in a cold cup to have lukewarm water poured upon them. When I called these teabags lingerie, I was attempting a little joke, a little joke, nothing more. I assure you, nothing more.'

I gazed out of the window and stared at a great wisteria the woven branches of which caught the light and turned it into patines as large as saucers upon the ground. I was waiting for a far-away look to come into my eyes to prove my innocence.

Suddenly the spirit lamp blazed up and overflowed upon the tray. The servant rushed forward and attempted to blow it out. The flames spread. He put his face down lower and blew.

'Hammond, leave the room!' Surprised, and leaving the mild conflagration behind him, the man obeyed. Quietly she continued the conversation where it had been broken off.

'Tea bags? I never heard of such things. They are not used in Charleston.' Her eyes swept the table where the fire was subsiding. I thought how awful it would be if the tea caddy were to blow up and a bag with 'Orange Pekoe' on a bright label pop out. Hammond's tenure would be short were that to occur.

'And now tell me,' she said in a sweet and gracious voice, 'How long are you staying in Charleston? Some of my friends are coming to dinner on Thursday night.'

'I have to leave to-morrow. I am awfully sorry.'

'You cannot have seen much of the town.'

'I have seen the best part of it.' I looked meaningly at the broad and polished boards with which the room was floored, old boards which had felt the touch of many a light and slippered foot and reflected many a silken stocking or jewelled sword hilt.

How shall I phrase my next remark so as delicately to convey a compliment? I wish to let her know that I have seen all that represents Charleston's traditions of grace and courtliness in her house. It would hardly do to say tritely, 'I have seen all I want, having had the pleasure of this visit.' Too obvious. There would be nothing of the grand manner about a phrase like that. I was at a loss. I could not rise to the noble and courtly days of old.

'This is the most interesting and charming city I have been in since I visited the United States,' I said. She inclined her head. 'What interests me,' I went on, 'is that the town is (let me see now, "embraced" might be misconstrued after my *faux pas* with "lingerie." I had better say "enclosed") enclosed by two rivers, the Ashley and the Cooper which is the hyphenated name of some acquaintances of mine, daughters of Lord Shaftesbury who got the concession or whatever they called it of Charleston. Ashley-Cooper is the family name of Lord Shaftesbury after whom the famous Shaftesbury Avenue in London is called.'

'And who had not the common courtesy to visit his "concession" as you call it.'

Again the whiff of Arctic air.

There are situations in which you find yourself where everything you say is misunderstood and out of which you may

159

not hope to emerge without falling deeper into the morass. I made a drastic effort.

'This is the most interesting and charming city I have been in since I visited the United States,' falling back on repetition.

'And how many have you been in?' she asked frigidly.

'About seventy,' I was able to reply. While that was sinking in, I rose to go. 'And what is a charming feature,' I added, 'it has not been deformed by those steel soap boxes superimposed one on the other which they call sky-scrapers in New York.'

'The North has not left us enough money with which to be vulgar,' she answered icily.

I was out, only just in time!

Women With Charm

Every little suburban village I have seen in the East of the USA appears like a town in Fairyland, or, rather, as a town would appear were I Mayor of Fairyland. The shining houses with their gaily painted walls and bright shutters, the smooth lawns and flowering trees keep up the illusion that they are inhabited not by hum-drum people but by folk of some magical society who at the waving of a wand might all vanish away. Of course, if you wish to think like that it is necessary to banish from your mind the pedestrian knowledge that the villages are not the result of magic but of standardization, landscape gardeners, seed catalogues and seeds as well as of public opinion which constrains each house-holder to trim his plot. The village corporation takes care of the leafy streets. Heaven takes care of the climate; and it takes a visitor from the first air-port where clouds land in Europe after crossing the Atlantic to appreciate the climate and to give it its need of praise.

Greenwich Village, Connecticut, is built on a series of knolls. Maybe it is not, but the part I visited seemed to be. Perhaps, as has often happened before, I found myself, by following an inclination which seems to be innate in my nature, in the part where the best people dwell. Out of consideration for popular and democratic opinion I have tried to correct this lamentable trait which can be so easily confused with snobbery but my efforts arouse feelings of hypocrisy when I pretend to enjoy plain people and unpleasant places.

So I bowl along in a sumptuous automobile and presently undulate up and down little hills on the top of which, gabled high, stand bright houses like so many high-roofed chateaux in La Belle France. Clean rocks covered with creepers jut out from the close green lawns and now I catch glimpses of water and lose the sight before I can make out whether it is the sea or a lake. I would engage the chauffeur in conversation if I could be sure that I could get him out of it when he had satisfied my curiosity. I cannot be sure so I refrain. It is much safer not to speak to the man at the wheel particularly for me. I am a chatty sort of person and if I were to talk to him he might begin to gesticulate as the conversation gathered interest and we might end up on the side of the tarmac still talking. So I resign myself to the lack of information and cease to wonder about the water so charming it is to be borne along with the light that falls from the rocky trees flickering across the sight.

Who lives in these hill-top houses? I shall know presently. I shall meet half their inhabitants for it is to a committee of ladies I have to yield myself up. I shall lunch with the ladies and then discuss subjects of aesthetic interest. I hate the word lecture with its suggestion of a lectern. I am going to a *conference* if that is the French for what is meant by lecture in the United States. As I have revealed I am about to address an audience of women. I have long ago given up addressing male audiences for many reasons. One reason is that it is only women who have time or the inclination for cultural subjects and (I will take the risk and say it) the understanding for themes which delight the mind. Another reason is that male audiences are hard to find. The men are busy turning deserts into production plants and when they have a moment in which to relax from their genius for organization they don't want to hear me but they want me to hear 'this one.' Having heard every one, I particularly don't want to hear 'this one.' Women never want to hear it. That is why I enjoy talking to them. Only the women preserve culture in the USA. Any trace of it that reaches the men reaches them through women. This is not to say that there are no professors, specialists and scholars in the country. Of course there are and they are more numerous here than in any country; but they do not form themselves into audiences for *belles lettres* and, besides, they know too much for me.

The car stops. I thought it was the country club but it is a private house with large rooms and pleasant furniture. No talking is pleasanter than talking in a private house. And this is a deep and cosy place. It is not one of those houses on its own little hill, one of those houses that makes you wonder how it would feel to wake up in the morning in the stillness just before sunrise. What sights you might see in the shadowless light before the sun had put mystery out of the world; what stately beings, what figure in a casement on the other hill. But those houses are not for us and the light we must live in is the light of day.

When I spoke of charm I said that it could exist without

162

physical beauty and was to be found amongst the old. That is true, but the existence of a rare type of beauty and the absence of old age do not necessarily banish charm. Distinction, an indescribable distinction of manner without aloofness, and a kindness that was evident in attentiveness and a residing smile were the influences that made up the spell. The woman had a kind and happy soul. That could be felt as well as perceived. Her intelligence had nothing to do with it though it, of course, did no more dispel it than her comeliness did. There was a certain straightforwardness about her speech and the way she stood, a simplicity of attitude and dress. I was curious about the sheet of water which I thought I had seen through the waving boughs.

'I am not sure if it was water. Water is indispensable from any landscape, even the desert has its mirages,' I said. Her companions waited for her to talk. What had I done? There was some little awkwardness in the air. Had I been overpraising the place? It would be hard to do that to the part of it that had been revealed to me. She smiled and stood with the simplicity of a Puritan maiden.

'Water,' I continued. 'But I could not be sure. Once when I thought I saw a lake in the distance it was only a half-hidden galvanized roof.'

'My house stands beside it,' she said. So it is water. I was right after all. 'I like to live beside water. I was born upon the bank of a river that ran through the town,' I remarked, but I had not quite dispelled the mystery. 'Is there anything wrong with the water?' I was sorry that I asked that, for it was perfectly obvious that these were people who were sufficiently endowed with the world's goods to choose the location of their homes.

'Oh, no.' She smiled, and the others laughed. Now I was being mystified. I was charmed already. Slight as the subject was, it was not light enough to blow away. It was something in me that they were sparing.

'Do tell me?' I prayed, and I took good care not to smile, for I never can tell what the effect might be. One of the committee spoke.

'She is afraid to tell you. After all your praise of words and places, she does not want to admit that her address is merely Steamboat Road.' I tried to look unconcerned, but not being a publisher I have not a poker face. Yet I could not enthuse over

Steamboat Road, that is with credible sincerity. I had been talking, as usual, too extravagantly. Then the charming lady spoke up.

'I think you are wrong about Steamboat Road.' She spoke to her friend and was referring to the supposed effect that name might have on me. 'It has a dour New England romantic touch about it that I relish.' Wishing to put her friend into it and to get myself out of any mistake there was, 'You are quite right,' I concurred. So she was aware of the dourness of New England romance and could appreciate it.

'We have boat yards, lumber yards, a slum, a yacht club, a dozen old houses behind walls, lilacs, apple blossoms and lobster pots in season. Always the smell of salt water and salt mud linger. I like it.'

This is New England directness, I realized. But what must they have thought of my efforts to discuss cultural subjects when they had so much cultural sensibility and minds that could see the beauty and romance behind the derelict things of everyday life and its haphazardness in their midst? A little disconcerting this New England awareness. Luckily, I had not tried to patronize or dictate to it. But oh, what simplicity, sincerity and Quaker charm.

The Life of Reilly

It is remarkable how much more than a mere word is required to convey an idea; and still more remarkable to recognize how much more than a mere statement is conveyed by additions to words which, without these aids, would be helpless to transmit emotion. Intonation, pitch, timbre, expression, nuance, gesticulation even, often do more to carry a message than the words themselves. The supreme example is rhythm, which is indispensable for the evocation of profound truths or hateful prophecies. The opposite of all this will exemplify my meaning: when you listen to an announcer on the radio with his deadly audible voice denuded of all charm, personality, sympathy or humanity, as unequivocal as a cash register, a dummy who has been taught to speak, you will see how helpless the toneless word is to express anything but publicity for a razor, tooth paste, a fur coat, dog food or a laxative.

When it comes to what can be conveyed by facial expression there is no limit. The first man to use the phrase The Life of Reilly to me was MacSpaddan whose ancestors were Scotch and must have come over with cases of it, if we are to judge by their descendant who lifts a consistent elbow when he discusses divinity or The Critique of Pure Reason which he is inclined to do on Sundays and holidays when the bank in which he works is closed. He made the remark when I enquired about an acquaintance of ours who had given up work. 'He is living the life of Reilly,' MacSpaddan said. It was the tone in which he said it that brought to me more facts, innuendos and conjectures than the words by themselves could possibly have conveyed. The first thing I felt (and don't think I was imagining it) was that MacSpaddan disapproved of Reilly's way of life. Mac is as upright and as honorable as Scotsmen usually are; but he is a little too exacting in his requirements about conduct especially when it comes to condoning extravagance; and his tone attributed many extravagances to Reilly's conduct of affairs. Among other things, I sensed the implication that Reilly had not earned the ease and luxury that were attributed to his life, but that he had come into them through no merit of his own – a windfall probably, or a winning ticket in the Irish Sweep or the sale of a tavern which had suddenly become valuable owing to the expansion of the Rockfeller Center, shall we say? Or the Dry Dock Savings Bank. I do not know how I came to get this last impression but I felt and I still feel that at one time or another before his life became proverbial Reilly was engaged in the liquor trade. One of the names of Bacchus was The Loosener because wine freed you from all care and restrictions. Reilly certainly was carefree. I was filled with a great wish to meet Reilly and to study his *modus vivendi*. That he is not engaged in the liquor trade now must be obvious to all and sundry who realize that work of any kind is inconsistent with the unbounded freedom from all effort, duties or concerns which the life of Reilly implies.

Having disassociated Reilly with work of any kind he became clearer under my eyelid. I see him as a man in the early fifties who weighs about 180 and looks like Christmas Eve. He carries a cane with a ferrule of light horn and an agate handle. His necktie is not 'conservative.' There is very little about Reilly that is. His signet ring is large; so, too, are his watch and expanding wrist band. His yellow gloves caught my eye and, just as I recognized the Reilly of my mind, he disappeared through a swing door. He was a little gaudy; but not aggressive. I remember saying to myself that if the representatives of the United Nations were all Reillys, we could feel safe.

Had MacSpaddan been an Englishman, he would have known that one of the English poets (all of whom were aristocratic until the Puritans came along), Henry Howard, Earl of Suffolk, commended as best the life that depended for its ease, not on 'got with care,' but on an inheritance. Reilly would have been more acceptable to an Englishman who can contemplate even a little wistfully a life without labor, than to a Scotsman who is liable to confuse ethics with industry.

I got another impression that amounted to a foreboding: It was this – that, at the pace he was going, Reilly could not last. Let me at once disabuse the reader's mind from anxiety; Reilly is, as far as I know, still going strong. I know that for a fact, for it is fully twenty years since MacSpaddan first alluded to Reilly's conduct of 'life's taper,' and only the other day I heard his life spoken of again without a hint of let-up or hindrance to his career. I grant you that it may be argued that Reilly is no more. If you will tell me how a man's life can be separated from his existence, I will come with you to the gloomy conclusion that Reilly is dead. Diamond Jim Brady in his day came very near to the way of life which is associated with Reilly. None of all those who may have envied Jim's exemplary conduct speak of him now, simply because he has passed away. So when you talk of the life of Reilly, at least concede that he is alive, for in the grave he would be forgotten lang syn – as MacSpaddan would say.

I know that MacSpaddan will concede grudgingly that Reilly is alive. MacSpaddan hopes some day that Reilly will collapse. To such a calamity he would point a moral. It must be aggravating for him to have to contemplate a career that has lasted so long without taking thought for the morrow. As I have remarked, Mac is somewhat of a philosopher and religiously inclined. I say this even though he does not scruple his ill will towards Reilly and all Reilly's pomps. Mac's wish for an end to Reilly may arise from the Unconscious; and, of course, no one is accountable for what goes on in there. To live at ease one must have a good conscience. For Reilly there is no nagen bite of in-wit. MacSpaddan had nothing to say to that. I am not at all sure that my attempts at a philosophical justification of the life of Reilly have not estranged me from MacSpaddan. He has not swum into my ken for a long time. I think that he suspected that my sympathies were with Reilly from the first. I will admit that there is something not altogether unpleasing to me in the contemplation of the prognostications of the rigidly righteous turning out to be wrong. For instance, it gives me much satisfaction to think that Buck Whaley, one of the 'Bucks,' spendthrifts, gamblers, and magnificent wastrels of the Eighteenth Century, instead of dying in a debtors' prison impoverished, died in affluence on the Isle of Man. That must have hit the Holy Willies hard, whose God would make the world not fit to live in. As I said, I am not at all certain that my efforts to defend Reilly and my lack of disapproval did not hit Mac hard; especially my lack of disapproval. Who am I to disapprove of Reilly, or anyone else if it comes to that? It is the disapprovers who are the curse of the earth. You will wait a long time before you will hear anyone say of another, 'He is living the life of Volstead.' Oh, no! Volstead represented an antithesis to Life.

Reilly to my knowledge has been living his life (I wish I knew all its ways) for upwards of twenty years. From that we must conclude that a life that has gone on so long without disaster must have commended itself to the Master of Life who does not brook the undeserving long. Those who like to think that the undeserving get a short shrift must agree with that. They will agree grudgingly when they realize it implies that there is something meritorious in Reilly's life. There is merit in all that is in harmony with the life of the world, with universal Nature.

Now, when you look closely into Nature's ways you will find that waste is an outstanding and ubiquitous attribute. Waste is inescapable: the waste of drones in the hive; the superfluous seeds on the earth; pollen in the air and the multitudinous spawn in rivers and seas – vast loss of life that Life may live: Death as a means to Life! It is inscrutable and yet without waste life cannot go on. Bear this in mind before you blame Reilly for extravagance. It may be that that wasteful way of his has endeared him to the Master. I begin to see as in a glass that Reilly's way and the Master's way are in accord. That is the reason for Reilly's survival. When the question as to Reilly being alive or not came up, I confess that I was a little anxious because I knew that Reilly was no valetudinarian. Nothing that is conveyed by the expression, The Life of Reilly, points to that, much less to his being a hypochondriac. To those who are worrying themselves into the grave by taking care of their health, Reilly's robustness is repugnant. And yet to imitate his careless regime might be the making of them. Reilly stands for *mens sana in corpore sano*.

Another friend, Barney Campbell, who, like MacSpaddan, is of Scotch ancestry, told me that when he was in Cuba he heard of Reilly. That did surprise me. Reilly in Cuba! What could Reilly be doing in Cuba? Then the alarming thought struck me: is Reilly a victim of a lecture agent? I tried to still my fluttering heart. Can you imagine such a man as Reilly signing a 'contract?' Nothing could contract Reilly who lives amply and at large, not even the rosy terms of a lecture agent. I know that there are some lecture bureaux who could tempt anyone. They offer the prospective novice forty-five per cent of his own earnings and a loan which he must accept. Then they flatter him by making him get himself photographed. This costs only $25. I know because the photographs which I already had proved unsuitable so I had to be photographed over again. It was explained to me that I was very lucky because the photographic artist was a close friend of the agent and the agent would see that I got a fair deal. That was one thing which consoled me about Reilly. I could not see him accepting a loan. He would have lent a deserving habitué five or ten on a cold night; but I could not see him borrowing from a lecture bureau. What confirmed me in my opinion that no lecture agent had got hold of Reilly was the third degree to which he would have to submit. He would have to have his voice changed to one such as I have described where all individuality disappears and at the end of a course in voice production Reilly would sound about as persuasive as a gutted herring. No lecture-voice for Reilly. At last the probability that Reilly was down in Cuba choosing his own cigars drove all the misgivings and apprehensions which the lecture agent caused out of my head. A great relief! The life of a human projectile which the lecturer has to live while working for the agent is the antithesis to what is meant by Reilly's attitude of slippered ease.

I have a way of putting types to the test. I multiply them by a million. I ask myself would the world be a happier resort with a million Volsteads or a million Reillys. It might be tolerable with a million MacSpaddans except on Sundays and holidays; but with a million Reillys – comely and pleasant all the time? Obstinacy, persistence, bigotry, scheming and meanness are not to be thought of in Reilly, whereas there are many I could name who exhibit the characteristics just mentioned. I cannot hear Reilly saying, 'Thou shalt not,' though I can hear him asking, 'What will you have?'

This anti-Puritanism is only to be expected in Reilly whose ancestors suffered from the hypocrisy and greed of Oliver Cromwell. Liberality in Reilly is bred in the bone.

I take a pride that amounts to patriotism when I think of Reilly's ancestors as countrymen of mine. It is to men of the stamp of Reilly that the world owes much of its geniality, the spirit of live and let live even if we cannot equal the life. I find myself using Reilly as a test or touchstone for character. I avoid those whose tones are disparaging or disapproving when they refer to his life. I would like to go round asking prominent men, 'What do you think of Reilly?' Then I would get all the slant I wanted, if I really could care what some of them thought.

Here a serious consideration must be faced. The old question of Epicurianism. Epicurus, as you know, held that Pleasure was the aim of existence. His garden was frequented by all who were neither Stoics nor ascetics nor bank managers. And why did that garden not verge on the light supreme? Because there were few who could take it. Take what, you will ask. Pleasure. They wanted, like men too exclusively married, to be corrected and nagged. They wanted Pain. The pleasure of some of them was to inflict pain on others. They dared not enjoy themselves. They had thrown in the sponge. They had declared life not worth living. They had despaired because they had given life too much thought. That is where Reilly comes in. He restores the relish of life. He aligns men's souls with the universal harmony. In meditating on the life of Reilly as I do for a few moments every day, that saying of Spinoza comes to mind: 'The free man contemplates life, not death.' There are so many cases of delayed burial and slow suicides on this earth that Reilly is indispensable if decent men are to live, men who are not afraid of life, not afraid to enjoy themselves, men with a good conscience.

I had not seen MacSpaddan twice in two decades. I met him one day after an organ recital. Wouldn't it have been just too good if Reilly were at the organ! But the thought was incredible. Reilly like myself enjoys music with resignation. I mentioned Reilly. This time he must have caught, as I did long ago from his, an impression from my tone of voice. 'You once told me of Reilly,' I said. 'Have you met him since? I have been trying to meet him for twenty years.'

Mac tilted his head sharply but did not look at me. He started to walk faster. 'You have not far to seek,' he said. '*You* are Reilly; and so is anyone who cannot thole discipline.'

Well! I'm . . . Reilly! Can you beat that?

American Patrons and Irish Poets

It has been said that seven cities claimed Homer when he was dead, the same cities through which, when living, he begged his bread. Whatever the factual truth or untruth of this statement, it illustrates a deep irony in the lives of a majority of poets: not only does recognition come most readily when monetary expressions are no longer necessary, but poetry and earning are, it seems, eternally opposing faculties. It may be that there has to be a certain fecklessness about a man who is susceptible to inspiration – the 'fine frenzy' of a poet is a bad qualification for a bank clerk, for instance; and it would never do for an engine driver to 'stand and stare.'

At any rate it is generally conceded that anyone who devotes his time strictly to 'meditate the thankless Muse' must have either private means, as Byron, Shelley, Browning and Swinburne had, or he must have a patron. Without patrons most poets would have to beg their bread as Homer did – or commit suicide as Chatterton did.

Patrons seem to have supported more than half the poets of history. Vergil was lavishly patronized by that most patient of men, the Emperor Augustus; Horace had Maecenas; and Dante, during one of his periods of exile, had the grudging Can Grande. Chaucer had not only a patron in John of Gaunt, but – what must be a boon to any poet – a document prohibiting any creditor from prosecuting him for debt. Thus, through literary history patronage has become the prerequisite of poets and the lack of patrons has become a very grievous thing. Dr Johnson adapted the line from Juvenal as an expression of his own sad experience –

This mournful truth is everywhere expressed;
Slow rises worth by poverty depressed.

His own experience in the worth of patronage undoubtedly brought him to the rescue of Oliver Goldsmith who was, for all his life, by poverty oppressed. It did not actually depress him; he had his natural Irish resilience to thank – and the early protection of the understanding Johnson, whose scathing rebuke to Lord Chesterfield for being merely a post-success patron of letters is known to everyone.

I think it was Gibbon who said that booksellers were the best patrons of literature. By booksellers he did not mean, of course, the keepers of stores and stalls for selling books, but what we now call publishers. Since Gibbon was a man of substance, he could afford to wait on his 'bookseller' for patronage; but if he had had to depend upon a modern publisher for the considerations of a patron, he would undoubtedly have written about his own decline and fall. This far from independent status of the poet hasn't changed throughout the years – the period from Goldsmith and Gibbon to Joyce and James Stephens is more distant in years than in economic characteristics. Patronage is no less essential today than it ever was; and perhaps the most distinctive feature of contemporary patronage is that appreciation and financial aid are coming to one nation of artists from another nation of admirers.

It would be a truism to say that no one can estimate all that Americans have done, morally, politically and militarily for Ireland through the centuries, nor can one picture what the present state of the country would be without such aid. The time has come for recognition of this help – more or less measurable, but still unacknowledged and partially unknown, which has been extended to the arts in Ireland – lest Ireland seem ungrateful.

In Ireland every great family used to have its poet. Before writing was common, it was up to the poet to record genealogies, achievements, marriages and deaths. He was a dependent of the family and the family was dependent upon him for its place in history. Therefore any notion of humiliation must be dissociated from the word 'patronage.' Poetry is, after all, no more self-supporting than is religion. And patronage, in either case, redounds as much to the patron's reputation as to that of the recipient.

From W.B. Yeats to Padraic Colum, there has not been an Irish writer of distinction who has not been heartened and helped by citizens of the United States. James Stephens, George Russell (AE) and James Joyce are all of this company.

Perhaps it all began back in 1901 when John Quinn, an eminent New York lawyer, read of an exhibition of paintings by Nathaniel Hone and J.B. Yeats, the father of the poet W.B. Yeats. The exhibit was organized by the late Sir Hugh Lane, the magnanimous art dealer, and George Moore wrote an introduction to the exhibition. Stimulated by Moore's comments, Quinn made his first visit to Europe and met the Yeats family in Bedford Park, London. He extended several commissions to the old portrait painter and bought ten of his son Jack's pictures. The timeliness of the gesture and old Yeats's appreciation were revealed in a letter in which he referred to Quinn as 'the nearest approach to an angel in my experience.'

From London, Quinn crossed over to Ireland where he met W.B. Yeats, Edward Martyn, Douglas Hyde and Martyn's cousin, the then somewhat aloof George Moore. He promised to arrange a lecture tour in the United States for W.B. Yeats and presented himself as exclusive purchaser of that poet's manuscripts. Yeats accepted and adhered scrupulously to this arrangement, as anyone who has tried to possess himself of a Yeats manuscript can testify.

In 1903 Yeats came to the United States for his tour, which brought him before many Irish societies, universities and colleges, including Bryn Mawr. While at that college, he wrote to his friend George Russell – and the letter is worth quoting for the signs it shows of his growing independence and self-confidence – attributes which America engendered in him and which it had been impossible for him to find in the circumstances under which he dwelt at home.

Dec. 8, 1903.

This is the chief women's college in America, the one to which the richer classes send their girls. I have just given my second lecture. I write to tell you of my success. At first I did not like my lecture at all. But last week I gave a lecture here which was, I thought, the best that I have given. It was on the intellectual movement. Last night I lectured again on heroic poetry and there was not standing room in the house. Not only the girls were there but a number of people from the neighbourhood . . .

One of the professors told me that I was the most 'vital influence' that had come near the college 'for fifteen years.' What has pleased me so much is getting this big audience by my own effort. They are getting all our books here now. Do you know I have not met a single woman here who puts 'tin tacks' in the soup. And I find that the woman who does is recognized as an English type. One teacher explained the difference to me in this way: 'We prepare the girls to live their lives but in England they are making them all teachers.'

John Quinn included in his arrangements for Yeats a lecture at Notre Dame. Of Notre Dame, Yeats, who was, when religious, a congenital Irish Protestant, wrote:

I have been entirely delighted by the big merry priests of Notre Dame – all Irish and proud as Lucifer of their success in getting Jews and nonconformists to come to their college, and of the fact that they have no endowments.

I gave four lectures in one day and sat up late telling ghost stories with the fathers at night. They belong to an easygoing world that has passed away – more's the pity – but certainly I have been astounded at one thing, the general lack of religious prejudice I find on all sides here.

It is evident from these letters that not the least appreciated advantage offered to Irishmen by American patrons is the opportunity to experience American intellectual civilization at first hand. And such contact, almost of necessity, works both ways. Yeats brought a knowledge of Ireland, its arts and aspirations, to thousands who had never before associated that country with anything but politics. He made magnificent use of his opportunity, making such friends for Irish literature as Henry James and President Theodore Roosevelt.

According to J.M. Hone's biography, while at Yale, Yeats 'made the remark quoted and considered as perverse in London, that American humor differs from English in its good nature; and he returned with glowing accounts of the intellectual alertness of American women.'

As a matter of fact it would be ungrateful as well as ungracious for one to consider the influence of American patrons on Irish poets without paying tribute to the women's clubs and poetry societies throughout the United States. In these the lecturer finds both appreciation and understanding. The intellectual alertness of American women to which Yeats referred is outstanding. The universities, colleges, clubs and poetry societies with which they are affiliated are the chief repositories of American culture. (This is a reversal of the cultural life of Europe in which women have no such share.) It may be that they have more leisure than the American men; but to what effect do they turn that leisure? They read more and write more books than the men. Literature depends on them. The truth of this statement will be apparent to anyone who considers what would become of the numerous magazines, novels and periodicals in the United States if women ceased to interest themselves in their production. It is they who demand information. It is their interest in the arts that makes it possible for the lecturers of foreign countries to find a living in the United States. In intellectual pursuits they are preeminent. To the women of the United States every poet should pay his grateful tribute.

To avoid any suggestion of gift-giving in patronage, it should be explained that Yeats was most scrupulous about monetary transactions. He endeavored to avoid indebtedness and to give full value for what was received. On his own part, Quinn was a shrewd bargainer. At least, his simple, unbusinesslike procedure of sending a sum of money, depending upon the liberality of the poet to return the money's worth in kind, developed into considerable 'profit.' For instance, by paying for an operation on James Joyce's left eye($200) he got in return the complete 1200-page manuscript of *Ulysses* in Joyce's clear and incisive handwriting. At the auction of Quinn's collection in 1924, the manuscript was sold for $1,975.

What neither Yeats, Joyce, nor any other poet could repay to their patrons was the knowledgeable sponsorship of their work and the introduction to the most hospitable country in the world.

The notice of a picture exhibition in Ireland attracted John Quinn to his career as a patron; on the other hand, the late Judge Richard Campbell introduced himself into the circle of patrons by putting up $2,700 to finance an exhibition of paintings by Irish artists at the Helen Hackett Gallery in New York. Through the exhibit, George Russell (AE) was brought over to America in 1930. Judge Campbell introduced him to Dr W. J. Maloney, the man who first conceived the plan for getting the White Cross to distribute ten million dollars throughout Ireland while that country was being devastated by the Black and Tans. On a second visit, Russell met Mrs Harriman Rumsey, who lent him her studio in East 40th Street where he promptly established a Platonic Academy. She also lent him her secretary, and arranged meetings with members of the Roosevelt cabinet, notably Henry Wallace, whom AE advised on rural organizations and cooperative institutions on the pattern of those he had founded in Ireland. She also provided him with a substantial honorarium.

Whereas Yeats was content to accept his father's somewhat abstract ideas and theories about America and Americans, AE really came to see and feel the American scene. He never tired of praising the American confidence, that indefeasible and indefeatable belief in the future which is so potent that it can mold a future. More than Yeats, who felt rather than realized, Russell's eloquent writings testify to what he learned and found admirable in America. Through his work as a philosopher and economist, he was more in touch with the national being of America than was the poet.

They who knew George Russell well may have wondered why he left the United States to return to Dublin where men of letters live more or less as outlaws. He would have made a magnificent American. He was welcome all over the country. The answer is simply this; his loyalty to Sir Horace Plunkett, who appointed him editor of The Irish Statesman, and to his public for whom that paper was his pulpit. His love for his Irish friends could not let him live away from them. Unlike Yeats, he did not actually need the emoluments accruing from his trips. He could have made money for his modest needs by his pen and brush anywhere. And he did; but he felt it a patriotic duty to inculcate in his countrymen the same progressive spirit, the sense of larger humanism and the belief in its destiny which he found in America.

When AE returned to Dublin, his office in Merrion Square became one of the great meeting places of American visitors and Irish artists. He did more than any other Irishman to bring about an understanding of the political and intellectual problems and aims of his country. He and Yeats managed, finally, to lift Ireland above the slough of petty politics and bigotries and refound Dublin in Athenian air.

Another liberal, if comparatively unknown patron of Irish poets, was the late Cornelius Sullivan. Sullivan did his good by stealth and was not given a chance to blush. He endowed poetry for poetry's sake. Any attempts to give him presents in token of gratitude or good will gave him more pain than pleasure.

Even as an acquaintance of the poets he admired, I came in

for my share of his bounty. He could not understand how anyone who was associated with poets could differ from them even in such a detail as comparative affluence. One had to be careful about expressing admiration for anything while in his presence, because, if it were available, he would insist on making a present of it. To me he presented the most perfect extant copy of Walt Whitman's *Leaves of Grass* merely because I admired the good gray poet. The edition was listed in Maggs' catalogue at $2,625. He refused to take it back. Something similar occurred with a piece of Galway silver, that rarest of all Irish specimens of silver.

Sullivan was the patron of James Stephens and he made a wise choice. Stephens is the last and most lyrical of the lyric group that came out of Dublin. Howe, the Cincinnati bookseller, was another of the poet's admirers, but Sullivan was generous enough to share even the distinction of sponsoring James Stephens.

It was Sylvia Beach, an American girl then residing in Paris, who drew James Joyce into the ranks of great writers indebted to American patrons. Joyce had labored on his monumental volume of *Ulysses* for twenty penurious years without much hope of it ever seeing the light of publication. Miss Beach recognized the vast design of the work and took the considerable risk of putting it through the press. This was the turning point in Joyce's unhappy life. Fame brought him many admirers and helpers. In Zurich, a Mrs McCormick of the Chicago McCormicks gave him a gift of thousands of dollars. Another lady, a Miss Weaver, presented him with $150,000, the residue of which sum is in trust for his grandson. But it was Sylvia Beach who gave him what so many Americans have given to Irishmen – opportunity.

It is characteristic of the generosity of Americans that it is neither momentary nor spasmodic, but vigilant and continuous. In 1937 a Testimonial Committee was formed in New York, presided over by the late James A. Farrell, President of the United States Steel Corporation. It was organized by Dr. W. J. Maloney for the 'purpose of expressing in a practical manner the admiration and affection felt for the great poet and great Irishman (Yeats) by his American friends of Irish ancestry or birth.' A fund was established which ensured Yeats a moderate income for his declining years. But, as he was not in want as he had been almost all his life up to the time he won the

Nobel prize (most of which was lost by the too cautious investments of a financial friend) it took some diplomacy to get the poet to accept the generous testimonial.

The delicacy and tact of the Committee overcame any scruples Yeats may have had about taking money he did not absolutely need. Also, there was one motive, not known to the Committee, which may have influenced the poet's willingness to accept. His wife requested that the money be sent to Ireland in installments. The poet, like his celebrated ancestor, the Sailor John, was 'hungering for one voyage more,' and his wife feared that if he got $5,000 down he would sail to, of all places, Japan. So Dr. McCartan, a very active member of the Testimonial Committee, went to Ireland with an installment. So liberal was the sum and so touched was the poet by the kindness and remembrance of his American friends that he made the matter public at a banquet of the Irish Academy of Letters held in the Dolphin Hotel, August 7, 1937. Furthermore, he published at the Three Candles Press, Dublin, an eleven-page pamphlet, 'A Speech and Three Poems,' which he sent to the fifty members of the Committee. He wrote to one of its founders, James A. Healy:

> I said that I would thank the other subscribers later. I spoke of my renewed visits to the Municipal Gallery where my friends' portraits are – visits made possible, or at any rate easy, now that I could go by taxi. I spoke of my emotion in the gallery where modern Ireland is pictured and I said that I had a poem on this subject in my head and would send it to the subscribers.

In the years up to the nineteenth century, Ireland may be said to have been nearer to the Continent, to Australia, Spain, France and to 'the Lowlands low' where so many of her soldier sons, including the Wild Geese, went. More recently, Ireland, through American visitors' interest in Irish literature and art, has drawn closer to America.

In the old days, the chief cultural centers were on the Continent: but their influence on Ireland was intermittent and uncertain. It is otherwise with the influence of America on Ireland. Both countries speak the same language; they have much history in common; both have, on the one side, singular individual genius and detachment; on the other, generosity, enthusiasm and appreciation of the unworldly way. The visit of

178

an educated American to Ireland is heartening. The Irishman, utterly unappreciated in his own country, is confirmed in his faith that the pursuit of the beautiful and the transcendental is worth while; American vigor rouses his courage to deal with life and it rouses his anger against those in his own country who cause what Yeats called 'The beating down of the wise, and great Art beaten down.'

In Ireland there is no hope for the budding genius. He is left to rot in the slums while the politicians go on consolidating the positions from which they abuse power or, in their ignorance, misdirect it. The gifted Olivia Robertson's recent novel tells the realistic story of a consumptive boy with a natural gift for drawing who is allowed to die unaided in one of Dublin's numerous slums.

The story inspired a reviewer in *The Irish Times* to editorialize that:

> The Society that allows Peter Keegan to decay physically and mentally is wasting its resources in just as serious and direct a sense as by burning its wheat and pouring its milk into the sea. The Irish middle class, the present rulers of the country, are not fit to rule unless they realize that money spent on giving equality of educational opportunity is money productively invested.

The renewal of traffic with America, shut off during the war, causes the Irishman to hope that those in power may be shamed into improving or at least providing a facade of culture and decency.

The Irish man of letters is even denied, or rather avoids, recourse to lecture tours, that source of additional income which American authors find so reliable. The entire group of Irish lecturers lack money and are driven to depend upon the liberality, in fact the charity, of private citizens of the United States. The reason is simply stated: the devastating rapacity of American lecture agents. These bureaucrats (they operate from 'lecture bureaus') charge 50 per cent of the lecturer's fees. There are charges quite outside the terms of the contract for 'publicity,' including as much as $25 for photographs. If the lecturer is a greenhorn, he may be sent to a voice director to learn how to speak in the dreadful, dehumanized and deadly audible tones so familiar to the commercial air waves. Worse than the downright 'fifty-percenters' are those agents who charge only 45 per cent but leave the lecturer to pay the train fares, then railroad him all over the union.

Few agents abide by their contracts and most will resort to trumped-up charges in order to inflict more of the financial burden upon the lecturer. There have been cases in which a cable reaches the lecturer just as he is aboard ship or plane demanding that an agreement on $5,000 be reduced to $3,700 on account of 'few responses to the (agent's) campaign' for the lecturer.

Misassociations are another painful experience, such as the instance in which the victim of his overzealous agent found himself lecturing on Shelley's 'Skylark' to the Hod Carrier's Union – and at a cut below the minimum arranged. This is usually timed for the end of the tour when the lecturer is too exhausted to defend himself. Frequently, in addition to all the other costs over and above the terms of the contract, there remains the necessity of employing an attorney to handle the lecture bureau. The situation in America is distinctly removed from that in Ireland, of course, but even though they include lectures to the afore-praised women's clubs and poetry societies, American lecture agents can hardly be included among the American patrons of literature.

The patrons of Irish poets have differed from each other as all men differ in character. They differ as John Quinn differed from Cornelius Sullivan. But the results of their patronage have been wholly healthy and productive. Returns on the part of all the Irish have not been as grateful as they should have been. There is something of the proverbial Indian beggar in every Irishman. In some parts of India a beggar thinks he is conferring a favor upon the man from whom he accepts alms because by accepting them he is permitting his benefactor to build for himself a more substantial reward in heaven.

Whether thanked with personal gratitude or not, the citizens of the United States who have encouraged the arts of Ireland, through their counsel and money have built for themselves an enduring monument.

To men like Dr Maloney, Judge Campbell, John Quinn, Cornelius Sullivan, Major Kinkead, James A Healy, James A Farrell, Dr McCartan and others, Ireland owes her rehabilitation as one of the centers of the world's culture. They helped to rip aside the age-long veil of misrepresentation of Ireland as an island full of drunken and pugnacious peasants that would tear itself to pieces but for the tolerant rule of the British Government. Ireland was revealed once more as Tir nan Oge, the Land of the Ever Young where imagination does not age nor business cloy its dream of beauty and perpetual invention. These are the American patrons who revealed the poetry of Ireland, who worked for and paid for that revelation and to whom the praise and thanks of those so liberally helped are due.

MARGARET RUTHERFORD

A Blithe Spirit

DAWN LANGLEY SIMMONS
Margaret Rutherford's adopted daughter

Margaret Rutherford, Britain's best-loved character actress, began her acting career at the surprisingly late age of 36. She made up for her late start both in quality and quantity, creating the classic comic roles of Madame Arcati in *Blithe Spirit*, Miss Prism in *The Importance of Being Ernest* and Miss Marple in the Agatha Christie films. Yet all her life Margaret Rutherford was the incurable romantic who never got to play Juliet – a passionate, innocent woman, haunted by the private terrors of madness, murder and suicide which had stained her family. Work was the only antidote, and Margaret triumphed over her personal difficulties to win an Oscar in the 1960s, achieving an everlasting place in our national affections.

'To read this book is to experience anew a cherished old love affair.'
STANDARD.

'The dark and sometimes sad side of a brave lady who brought laughter to the rest of us.'
DAILY MAIL.

'A straightforward and warm-hearted study of a much-loved woman . . . more than that, it's a very human comment on a very special being.'
WOMAN'S JOURNAL.

BIOGRAPHY   0 7221 7861 1   £1.95

*Time is running out for the savage splendour
of Imperial China . . .*

MANDARIN

Robert Elegant

Creator of DYNASTY and MANCHU

After the First Opium War of 1840, China is in turmoil. In the
South, insurrection threatens; in Shanghai, 'barbaric' Western
influence is spreading – and on all sides, the dazzling old
world of the Orient faces the onslaught of the new . . .

Against the gorgeous and turbulent panorama of Imperial
China under the Great Pure Dynasty of the Manchus,
MANDARIN unfolds an epic adventure of revolution and
romance, peopled by a glorious cast of characters – warriors
and lovers, concubines and courtiers, seekers of fortune in war
and in trade . . . the merchant Saul Haleevie, bidding for
power alongside the great European trading houses; Fronah
his daughter, torn between love and virtue; and the
unscrupulous Yehenala, whose destiny would one day be
inextricably linked with that of China itself.

MANDARIN magnificently recreates China at a momentous
turning point in its colourful history: a sweeping, spectacular
drama – vast yet intimately human – of an exotic world that
was to vanish forever.

'A huge tale . . . full of romance, exoticism and
danger.' *Good Housekeeping.*

FICTION/GENERAL   0 7221 3275 1   **£2.95**

A SELECTION OF BESTSELLERS FROM SPHERE

FICTION

SMART WOMEN	Judy Blume	£2.25 ☐
INHERITORS OF THE STORM	Victor Sondheim	£2.95 ☐
HEADLINES	Bernard Weinraub	£2.75 ☐
TRINITY'S CHILD	William Prochnau	£2.50 ☐
THE SINISTER TWILIGHT	J. S. Forrester	£1.95 ☐

FILM & TV TIE-INS

WATER	Gordon McGill	£1.75 ☐
THE RADISH DAY JUBILEE	Sheilah B. Bruce	£1.50 ☐
THE RIVER	Steven Bauer	£1.95 ☐
THE DUNE STORYBOOK	Joan D. Vinge	£2.50 ☐
ONCE UPON A TIME IN AMERICA	Lee Hays	£1.75 ☐

NON-FICTION

THE *WOMAN* BOOK OF LOVE AND SEX	Deidre Sanders	£1.95 ☐
PRINCESS GRACE	Steven Englund	£2.50 ☐
MARGARET RUTHERFORD – A BLITHE SPIRIT	Dawn Langley Simmons	£1.95 ☐
BARRY FANTONI'S CHINESE HOROSCOPES	Barry Fantoni	£1.75 ☐
THE STEP-PARENT'S HANDBOOK	Elizabeth Hodder	£2.95 ☐

All Sphere books are available at your local bookshop or newsagent, or can be ordered direct from the publisher. Just tick the titles you want and fill in the form below.

Name_____

Address_____

_____

Write to Sphere Books, Cash Sales Department, P.O. Box 11, Falmouth, Cornwall TR10 9EN

Please enclose cheque or postal order to the value of the cover price plus:

UK: 55p for the first book, 22p for the second book and 14p per copy for each additional book ordered to a maximum charge of £1.75.

OVERSEAS: £1.00 for the first book and 25p per copy for each additional book.

BFPO & EIRE: 55p for the first book, 22p for the second book plus 14p per copy for the next 7 books, thereafter 8p per book.

Sphere Books reserve the right to show new retail prices on covers which may differ from those previously advertised in the text or elsewhere, and to increase postal rates in accordance with the PO.